D1607519

Off the Record

Off the Record

Country Music's Top Label Executives Tell Their Stories

JENNIFER EMBER PIERCE

MADISON BOOKS
Lanham, New York, Oxford

Published by Madison Books
4720 Boston Way
Lanham, Maryland 20706

12 Hid's Copse Road
Cumnor Hill, Oxford OX2 9JJ, England

Distributed by National Book Network

Library of Congress Cataloging-in-Publication Data

Pierce, Jennifer Ember.
  Off the record: country music's top label executives tell their stories / Jennifer Ember Pierce.
    p. cm.
  Includes bibliographical references and indexes.
  ISBN 1-56833-148-7 (alk. paper)
  1. Country music—History and criticism. 2. Sound recording executives and producers—Interviews. 3. Sound recording industry—United States. 4. Music trade—United States I. Title.

ML3524 .P54 2000
781.642'149'092273—dc21
[B]   99-050264

To my brothers, Ted and Dave

Contents

Acronyms

ABC	American Broadcasting Company
A&R	artists and repertoire
ACM	Academy of Country Music
AF of M	American Federation of Musicians
AFTRA	American Federation of Television and Radio Artists
ASCAP	American Society of Composers, Authors and Publishers
ADAT	Alesis Digital Audio Tape
BDS	Broadcast Data Systems
BMI	Broadcast Music Incorporated
BMG	Bertelsmann Music Group
BNA	Berry Field/Nashville Airport
CBS	Columbia Broadcasting System
CD	compact disc
CEO	chief executive officer
CMA	Country Music Association
CMI	Copyright Management Inc.
CMT	Country Music Television
DAT	digital audiotape
DRD	double record
EMI	Electric and Musical Industries, Ltd.
EP	extended play
H&W	health and welfare
LP	longplay album ($33^1/_3$-speed record)
MCA	Music Corporation of America

MCG	Mike Curb Group
NARAS	National Academy of Recording Arts and Sciences
NBC	National Broadcasting Corporation
NEA	Nashville Entertainment Association
RCA	Radio Corporation of America
RLG	RCA Label Group
RPM	revolutions per minute
R&R	Radio & Record
SAG	Screen Actors Guild
SESAC	Society of European Stage Authors and Composers
SKB	Schuyler, Knobloch and Bickhardt
SKG	Spielberg, Katzenberb and Geffen
SONY	derivation Latin; Sonus = (sound)
TNN	The Nashville Network
UA	United Artists
VH1	Video Hits 1
WEA	Warner/Elektra/Atlantic

Explanatory Note

Square brackets are used when it is necessary for the author to explain, clarify, or expand on certain passages in the text.

The lists in the backmatter are not intended to be all-inclusive and are subject to change.

Brief definitions have been placed in the body of the text rather than in the introduction or backmatter so as not to interrupt the flow of the chapter by causing the reader to stop and search through other portions of the book for relevant definitions. Longer explanations are contained in the glossary section.

Certain viewpoints expressed in this book do not necessarily reflect those of the author.

Figures and amounts reflecting monies paid or earned in the music industry by various artists, executives, musicians, and so on are always subject to change in accordance with the normal rise and fall of the economy.

The word *he,* when used nonspecifically, is intended to reflect both genders.

There is a great deal of rapid turnover in the music industry; therefore, some addresses in the List of Addresses may have changed; some record companies may have moved to another geographical location, others may have gone out of business, and new record companies may have been formed.

Chapter formats may vary because some labels have a longer history; therefore, a brief history of the origin of that label appears prior to the chapter. Where the history does not appear prior to the chapter, that label's origin is incorporated within the chapter.

Foreword

Harold Bradley

*O*ff *the Record* covers, in detail, the inner workings of some of the major record labels in Nashville. This firsthand account from record executive interviews with the author will give the reader a close-up look into one of the biggest industries in the world—the music industry.

Each chapter includes a brief history of the label under discussion along with the executive's personal story. Covered in this book are Joe Galante, president of RLG (RCA Label Group); Mike Curb, president of Curb Records; Lynn Shults, who covers Capitol, United Artists, and Atlantic Records; Luke Lewis, president of Mercury Records; Danny Kee, A&R executive for Reprise Records; and James Stroud, director of DreamWorks Records, a company owned by SKG (Spielberg, Katzenberg, and Geffen). Both foreign and domestic markets are included, as are those who really own the record companies—that is, the chain of ownership and the distributors of the records on a worldwide basis.

If you have ever wondered how stars become stars, how records are really made, or what your chances are of becoming a major recording artist, this book is for you. You will read about how many famous artists got signed to label deals, and you will understand why careers come to an end. Questions are asked and answered regarding recording costs, studio selection, studio time, payment to session musicians and studio engineers, what percentages are paid to producers, how radio works with the labels, what type of personality one must have to be a recording artist in today's megamarkets, the most important personality traits necessary for continued success in the music industry, and how the various departments and divisions of the major labels function, including A&R (artists and repertoire), sales, promotion, publicity, and video.

The book tells a forthright tale, from the beginnings of certain artists' careers all the way to the completion of their first albums. The book provides an excellent overview and history of all sides of the recording industry, from the introduction of new artists to the pain of letting them go. No doubt will be left in the reader's mind as to how important record sales are to a label.

Jennifer Ember Pierce is well respected in the major music industry for her loyalty, honesty, and sincerity as she continues to write about all facets of the Nashville music industry. *Off the Record* should be on the desks or in the libraries of anyone who wants to really know "the true story" of the major Nashville record labels.

Acknowledgments

I want to thank my family: L. Wheeler Pierce and Sylvester Pierce; my nieces, Natalia Nero, Tara Turk, and Trina Silvergate; my brothers, Ted and Dave Turk; and my friends, Terry Bell, John E. Mann, and Cheryl, Nelson, Danny, and Richard Leclair.

I greatly appreciate the help of Tom Roland, music editor for the *Tennessean*, in developing the historical research for this book.

I also want to thank the following people: Wiley Alexander, the *San Antonio Express* and *News/STAR* magazine; Barry Beckett, Beckett Productions; Fran Boyd, executive director, Academy of Country Music (ACM); Carter Butler; Debi Champion, artist/songwriter; Tom Collins, Collins Music; Bruce, Susan, and Wes Conklin; Curt Conroy, author/songwriter; Jerry Cupit, Cupit Music; Shawn DeLorme, artist; Wayne DeLorme; Byron Gallimore, Pride Music Group; Bill Gatzimos, Gayle Enterprises, Inc.; Sonny George, artist/songwriter; Jack Gulledge, attorney; Jacqueline Gulledge, songwriter; Bill Hallquist, K-Tel Records; Rick Hogan, *American Songwriter* magazine; Buddy Killen, Buddy Killen Enterprises; Bob and Louise Lancer; Rick Malkin, photographer; Nikki Mitchell, business manager for Waylon Jennings; Clay Myers, creative services, artist development, and publishing; David Ross, editor/publisher, Music Row Publications, Inc.; Tony Sarno, artist/songwriter; Rob Senn, senior vice president and general manager, National Academy of Recording Arts and Sciences® (NARAS®); Jim Sharp, *American Songwriter* magazine; Tim Stacy, artist; David Stewart, author/songwriter; Bill Todd, Atlanta Police Department; Edith O. Toombs; Natalia Turk; Triona Murray Turk; Ron Twist, musician/songwriter; Allen Wernle, musician; and Jo Lynn Whaley.

A special thanks to Marla Burns, executive assistant to James Stroud, DreamWorks Records; Chris Carroll, executive assistant to Luke Lewis, Mercury Records/Nashville; Becky Judd, executive assistant to Mike Curb, Curb Records; and Jane Messmore, executive assistant to Joe Galante, RLG/Nashville.

Introduction

With few exceptions, Nashville recording stars are made, not born. This book, based on extensive interviews with top executives from some of Nashville's major recording companies, takes readers behind the scenes and provides a detailed description of the multi-billion-dollar business that creates recording stars. It is a high-powered, highly competitive, fast-paced world in which one will not become a star without the help of large amounts of well-spent money, including promotional budgets ranging up to a million dollars per artist. Making a star in today's worldwide marketplace involves a team effort by some of the world's most highly skilled musicians, songwriters, audio and video producers, engineers, executives, managers, and media specialists. This introduction explains a few features of the industry that will help the reader understand the chapters that follow.

Recording companies, referred to as *labels,* generally have divisions devoted to the major types of music that they produce, such as country, gospel, adult contemporary, alternative, and pop. Each division is a largely self-contained unit with a number of departments, including A&R (artists and repertoire), business, finance, international, production, marketing, promotion, publicity, publishing, sales, and video. Although most labels function in basically the same way, some may combine various departments and divisions. The functions of many of these departments do not require special explanation, but several are described here whose activities are not fully conveyed by their titles.

The A&R Department

At the center of the constellation is the artists and repertoire department. The A&R department is responsible for signing artists to the label. It coordinates with the label's executives, the artist, and the artist's manager to determine such matters as the best possible songs for the artist to record and strategies for marketing, publicizing, and promoting the artist.

It is rare that an artist simply walks into a label's offices and is signed solely on the basis of talent. Most artists are located and signed on the basis of a network of contacts within the music industry and the music world. Those in positions of power are likely to sign artists with whom they are acquainted or who have been recommended to them by someone they know and trust. As in many other fields, it also doesn't hurt to be married or related to the right person or to have important friends.

To be signed, an artist must exhibit more than musical talent. He must have the intangible quality of getting along well and being liked by a substantial assortment of persons, even including other artists who work for and are involved with the label. Craggy personalities, or even personalities who have the misfortune of arousing the dislike of one person, face obstacles that have little to do with musical ability.

The Artist's Advance

It is difficult for an artist to hold a full-time job while working on recordings. When an artist is signed, he or she may therefore receive an advance against future royalties to cover living expenses while recordings are being made and produced. Advances can run between $15,000 and $100,000, with most being about $25,000. These advances are designed to help the artist meet basic expenses for a period of six months to one year. Label executives exercise adequate caution, when necessary, to ensure that advances are used to cover such basics as rent, mortgage payments, and car payments.

In addition to the advance, the label pays all costs of producing the project and also pays for photographs and publicity spreads in newspapers and key trade magazines such as *Billboard*. The granting of advances and the payment of these costs involves the entire label in the artist's fortunes. After a period ranging from six months to one year, the artist is evaluated by the label's executives. If the artist succeeds, his record sales are used to repay his advances, and then he and the label share the rewards of the balance of the monies. If he does not succeed, the advances are absorbed by the label. However, the lengthy experience and know-how of the label executives reduce failure to a minimum.

Publishing Houses

Publishing houses are often affiliated indirectly with the labels. The function of publishers is to pitch their writers' songs to other major labels for their artists as well as to artists on the label affiliated with their own publishing house. For example, the publishing branch for Warner Bros. and Reprise Records is Warner/Chappell Publishing Company.

Staff writers may number from 40 to 100. All these writers are paid varying draws against future royalties on their songs, ranging from $50 to $500 a week. When a songwriter receives checks from ASCAP (the American Society of Composers, Authors and Publishers), BMI (Broadcast Music Incorporated), or SESAC (which once stood for Society of European Stage Authors and Composers but is now used only as its acronym) for airplay for his material, the labels first deduct the writer's draw and then distribute his check.

Publishing houses may function as wholly owned subsidiaries of the parent label and, theoretically at least, may operate with a degree of business independence. But while publishing companies may operate with some autonomy, it is obviously to the label's advantage to have its artists record songs that have been written by the label's affiliated publishing house, thereby keeping a larger portion of the revenues in-house. This may cause labels to choose songs for an artist that were written by writers at their publishing houses rather than better or more appropriate material that was written elsewhere. However, one would be hard-pressed to find a label executive who would admit to this practice. This inclination is reinforced, at least in part, by a belief that publicity and success in achieving airplay can compensate for any inferiority in the material.

Jobs as staff songwriters are secured usually by outside writers who already know one or more staff writers at the label's affiliated publishing house. Also, jobs may be acquired after an independent writer has had some success on his own.

As with recording artists, the ability to get along well with others is important. This is especially critical for staff writers, for valid reasons, because writers often work together to write songs. Staff writers are like families. The hiring of a new writer is discussed by all the staff writers or at least by those who have had the greatest success with their songs. If they do not like the proposed newcomer, he will not be signed.

The system can increase difficulties of access by independent songwriters. All staff writers are expected to collaborate with other staff writers. Unless an independent writer is willing to write his songs as coauthor or cocomposer with a staff writer or enjoys a special "in" with the company, the odds of his songs being used are greatly diminished.

When songwriters collaborate, the proceeds from licensing and royalties are split among the writers on the song. A glance at the country singles charts in *Billboard* magazine shows that as many as five publishers and two to five writers may be involved on the same song.

The Production Department

The artist's producer is selected by the label executives and the recording artist. The artist, his manager, and the label are jointly involved in making this decision. Depending on prearranged agreements among artist, manager, and producer, all are involved in making key decisions regarding the artist's career.

Usually, outside producers work in conjunction with key A&R people at the artist's label. Allen Reynolds, who produces Garth Brooks, among others, works with the A&R staff at Capitol Records when producing Garth. Independent producers are the norm because most aspiring artists have already worked with an independent producer prior to being signed to a label. Faith Hill was produced by Scott Hendricks, who then helped Faith get signed to Warner Bros. Records.

A few famous independent producers are: Jerry Kennedy, who produces the Statler Brothers; Allen Reynolds, who produces Garth Brooks, Kathy Mattea, and many others; Barry Beckett, who was an instrumental producer in the career of Hank Williams Jr.; and Byron Gallimore, who produces Tim McGraw and others.

Most of the time, an artist will have the help of a well-known independent producer or a well-known manager who helps the artist get signed to a major label. Bob Doyle, who owns the publishing rights to most of Garth's songs, left his executive position at ASCAP to become his manager back in 1987. Bob, along with co-manager Pam Lewis, producer Allen Reynolds, and key ASCAP executives, was instrumental in getting Garth signed to Capitol Records.

Independent producers lease studio space for recording. Polygram Island, the publishing house for Polygram/Mercury/MCA, has one of the finest state-of-the-art recording studios in the United States. All major studios in Nashville lease their studios for independent use. The cost can run as high as $2,500 a day. A big consideration in producing an artist is to record him in the best possible studio with the best engineers.

Independent producers are also advantageous in that they have produced hundreds of artists dealing with all genres of music; therefore, their vast experience is most welcome by the labels in dealing with new or established artists.

Most label executives who head up the labels or A&R departments were independent producers prior to coming to the label; however, once at the label, their expertise is in the A&R departments. Although they work with independent producers, their main function is overseeing every facet of an artist's professional career.

Videos

Where video departments exist, they work with independent video companies and independent video producers along with the A&R department to create music videos for the artist. The advent of music videos has impacted the music industry in many ways, including ways that may not necessarily foster the production of high-quality material. The business of producing recording artists has become increasingly visual and youth oriented. Marketing studies confirm that most record buyers are females between the ages of twelve and twenty-five. These buyers prefer to see videos of attractive young males. It is for this reason that the labels sign more male than female artists.

The Web of Ownership

Today, most major labels are owned by foreign-held parent companies. The following is a brief synopsis of the chain of ownership of some of the major labels in Nashville.

BMG (Bertelsmann Music Group): The publishing arm and parent company owns RLG (RCA Label Group), which consists of RCA Records (Radio Corporation of America) and BNA (an acronym for Nashville's airport, Berryfield Nashville Airport), Arista, and Career Records. The corporation is set up with well-defined lines, with RCA, BNA, Arista, and Career being freestanding labels.

While many Music Row observers tend to watch the activities of the individual record labels to determine which companies are winning the competition, a larger-level competition among the major distributors is perhaps even more important. The record label is the specific company that releases and markets a particular album, but the distribution company is the firm that makes sure the album gets into the record stores.

The largest distribution web in country music is WEA, which represents a bundle of different labels. Founded in the early 1970s by Warner Communications, Inc., WEA includes the following:

Warner Bros.: The central label in the chain, handles such acts as Travis Tritt, David Ball, Brady Seals, and Anita Cochran.

Elektra: Elektra remains a viable pop label, although the company is no longer active in country music. Founded by Jac Holzman on October 10, 1950, as a jazz and folk label, Elektra became a significant country contender in the mid-1970s, offering such acts as Hank Williams Jr., Eddie Rabbitt, Crystal Gayle, Conway Twitty, and the Bellamy Brothers. When Warner and Elektra merged in January 1983, Elektra chief Jimmy Bowen took over the expanded Warner Bros., and the Elektra logo was retrieved in country music.

Atlantic: Atlantic made a permanent move into country music in 1989, developing a roster that features John Michael Montgomery, Tracy Lawrence, and Confederate Railroad.

Asylum: When manager David Geffen shopped Jackson Browne to Atlantic Records in the early 1970s, unimpressed Atlantic chief Almet Ertegun told Geffen that if he was so psyched about the singer, he should start his own record company and put out records himself. Geffen did and brought the Eagles, Linda Ronstadt, and Joni Mitchell into his stable, too. He sold the company within a couple of years. Asylum earned a country hit in 1980, when Johnny Lee released "Lookin' for Love," though the label didn't make a concerted effort at country until 1992, when it opened a Nashville office for the first time, with Kyle Lehning in charge. The label introduced Lila McCann, Kevin Sharp, and Bryan White. In 1998, Evelyn Shriver took over the label, becoming the first female to be president of a major Nashville record company.

Giant: Founded in 1989 by the Eagles' manager, Irving Azoff, Giant jumped into the fray in Music City in 1991, releasing its first album, by Dennis Robbins, on April 1 of that year. With record producer James Stroud in charge, the label earned hits with Carlene Carter, Daryle Singletary, and Clay Walker, though its biggest success came with the three-million-selling *Common Thread: The Songs of the Eagles*, which earned a Country Music Association award for the album of the year in 1984. Stroud left in 1997 and was replaced by former Sony producer Doug Johnson, who's worked with Ty Herndon, and Doug Stone.

EMI (Electric and Musical Industries, Ltd.): The publishing arm and British-held parent company owns Capitol Records.

Polydor: The Amsterdam-based Dutch-held parent company owns Mercury Records/Nashville, which is owned by Seagram Company, Ltd. Its publishing house is Polygram Island.

Sony Music: The Japanese-held parent company owns Columbia, Epic, Monument, and Lucky Dog Records. Its publishing branch is Sony/Tree Music Publishing International.

MCA (Music Corporation of America): Along with Decca Records, MCA is owned by Seagram Company, Ltd., a global beverage and entertainment company. MCA Music is the publishing branch. In 1999, Seagram Company, Ltd., also purchased the Mercury/Polygram Label Group.

DreamWorks Records: A division of DreamWorks SKG, an entertainment company formed in 1994 by Steven Spielberg, Jeffrey Katzenberg, and David Geffen, DreamWorks is marketed through Geffen Records, which is owned by Universal Studios, Inc., a unit of the Seagram Company, Ltd.

Time Warner: The U.S. parent company owns Warner Bros., Reprise, Atlantic, Giant, and Asylum Records. The publishing arm is Warner/Chappell Music Publishing.

Nashville Labels

Nashville's status as a national and international hub of the recording industry is reflected in the large number of labels that have either their headquarters or branches of their home offices in the city. The following record labels make their home in Nashville: Aaron Records, Almo Sounds, Amethyst Records, Arista Records, Asylum Records, Atlantic Records, BNA Records, Bellamy Brothers Records, Blue Hat, Bransounds, Capitol Records/Nashville, Career Records, Columbia Records, Curb Records, Curb Universal, MCG/Curb, Dead Reckoning Records, Decca Records, DreamWorks, Elektra Entertainment, Epic Records, Giant Records, Heartland, Imprint Entertainment, Intersound Entertainment, Island Records, Justice Records, Little Chickadee Productions, Little Dog/Polygram, Lucky Dog Records, Lyric Street Records (a Disney Corporation), MCA/Nashville, Margaritaville Records, Magnatone Entertainment, Mercury Records/Nashville, Monument Records, Oh Boy Records, Platinum Entertainment, RCA Records, Red Pony Records, Rising Tide, River North/Nashville, SBK (Schuyler, Bickhardt and Knobloch; U.S./EMI Music Canada), Shiloh Records, Sugar Plum Records, Vanguard Records, Voyage Records, Warner Bros. Records, Reprise Records/Nashville, Watermelon Records, Work, Inc., and Zoo Records.

For a partial list of record companies, with addresses and phone numbers, see the List of Addresses toward the end of the book.

1

James Stroud

DreamWorks Records

There isn't any map on the road to success; you have to find your own way.
—Anonymous

About DreamWorks Records

The idea for DreamWorks was conceived at the White House. Steven Spielberg, Jeffrey Katzenberg, and David Geffen were having dinner with the president, and, as the conversation drifted into the realm of entertainment, the idea for DreamWorks was born.

DreamWorks has a huge publishing company in Los Angeles whose staff is busily writing the music for Spielberg's numerous hit movies. But Mo Ostin, who is an executive in the Los Angeles office, along with the above-named moguls, believed that Nashville, along with having the highest standards for creativity and product, would offer a wonderful and beneficial extension for their creative ideas.

As DreamWorks/Nashville came into being, no one was given a title because the Los Angeles owners do not believe in titles. They feel that titles cast an unequal light on company employees and that employees work together on a more equal basis without them.

DreamWorks/Nashville currently has some of Nashville's finest songwriters signed to the company: Steve Dorff, whose son Steven Dorff is an actor; Chris Lindsey, who has songs on albums by Deanna Carter and Tim McGraw; Rafe VanHoy, who is one of the finest writers in the Nashville music community; and Troy Seals, a veteran and proven writer.

It is hoped that the DreamWorks/Nashville operation will grow into other areas of entertainment along with the music. Over the years, Dream-Works is planning to become a huge entertainment entity in Nashville.

James Stroud

Early Years

I was born on July 4, 1949, in Shreveport, Louisiana. I have four siblings: Charlotte, Wanda, Guy, and Vickie. My mom and dad raised all of us on $300 a month. I had pretty amazing parents. My father, Walter, was an oil field worker, and he moved to where he could find work in the fields; so I was raised in both Louisiana and Texas.

I always loved music, as did all the members of my family, and I listened to the radio and records whenever I could. My mother, Ola Mae, was the musician in the family. She'd taught herself how to play the piano. She had a natural ability. I was fascinated with the drums, which I began playing when I was twelve years old, in the 7th grade in junior high school. Both my brother, Guy, and my brother-in-law, Shelton, played the drums in high school, and they inspired me to play. I began to play professionally when I was around sixteen years old.

While I was attending Woodlawn High School, my grandmother, Amelia, purchased a set of drums for me. I played those drums in the high school band. At halftime during high school football games, I would march forward, sit down at my drums, and play a couple of big-band tunes.

After graduating from high school in 1967, I began to play in Bossier City, Louisiana, and in some clubs around Black Lake in southern Louisiana, where no one had to worry about showing an ID, which worked for me because I was too young to be working in those clubs. I was playing six nights a week. I remember the first week I went to work: I made $80, which was more than my father made doing backbreaking work in the oil fields.

When I was eighteen years old, I played in a studio on some sessions in Shreveport, Louisiana, and in Jackson, Mississippi. I moved to Jackson when I was nineteen and played in more clubs and worked on more sessions. I was hired by Malaco Studios and played on my first hit records: "Groove Me" and "Mr. Big Stuff."

As I continued playing in various studios, I became interested in engineering and producing. I began to engineer recording sessions in 1972 at

Malaco Studios. I did engineering work for about ten years. I mixed the sound for the records and overdubbed instruments, vocals, and vocal harmonies. During this period of time, I also learned how to arrange music. So by the time I was twenty-two years old, I was arranging music, playing drums and percussion, and producing records.

My interest in engineering was born out of necessity. I was working in Jackson, at Malaco Records. There was a small nucleus of people who made all the records at Malaco. There were a couple of studio engineers, along with a studio rhythm section, who were all owners in the company. Eventually, because of growth, we ran out of manpower. When the two engineers were busy on other projects, I began to engineer some vocal tracks, then I went to instrumental tracks, and finally I learned how to mix the session. So I learned to engineer through trial and error.

I was also interested in becoming a recording artist. In 1975, Stax Records, which was located in Memphis, Tennessee, signed me to a demo deal. I was one of the few white recording artists on the Stax label. I sang on recordings for various songwriters and producers. However, Stax closed down soon after signing me.

In 1988, I was signed to Curb Records/Nashville. I was playing with a band called the Snakes at that time. I had learned to play percussion instruments as well as the drums and did quite a bit of studio work as a percussionist. As an artist with the Snakes, we toured with or opened for the Fabulous Thunderbirds and Nirvana.

The Majors

It all started in 1981 at Elektra Records in Nashville. I was doing some producing for Jimmy Bowen as well as working in the A&R department. Jimmy taught me quite a bit about how to structure an A&R department as well as how to deal with the artists on our roster.

In 1988–89, I became the director of A&R for MCA/Universal Records in Nashville. At that time, MCA and Universal were the same label. Jimmy Bowen was the CEO and president. In 1990 and 1991, both Bowen and I moved over to Capitol Records/Nashville, which was located on 16th Avenue. We were housed in the Lee Greenwood Building. I headed up the A&R department; Bowen was the head of the label. While at Capitol, I signed Pirates of the Mississippi. It was at this time I began to realize that I could play an integral part in the record industry as an executive. I stayed at Capitol for one year.

Thinking back, I believe I decided that I wanted to stay in the business end of the business from having worked at the above record labels and having worked with Garth Brooks when I was at Capitol Records. Garth had just been signed to Capitol by Lynn Shults, who was with Capitol's

A&R department. When I was head of A&R at Capitol, I worked with Garth on some of his earlier albums. Jimmy and I visited with Garth and explained to him what our ideas were to promote him and his music. Then I became involved with Garth and helped him with his video on "The Dance."

Working with Jimmy Bowen and Garth decided my future in the industry. I learned a lot about the business and felt that I could, in some small way, better the industry by staying in the business as an executive. I paid a lot of attention to the production side of the business and was quite successful.

Clint Black

I left Capitol in 1991 to devote my time producing Clint Black. At that time, Bill Ham was managing Clint. Bill Ham and Richard Perna, who was also working with Bill and Clint, came into my office to talk with me about producing Clint. Clint had previously talked with another producer, Kyle Lehning, but Kyle turned Clint down. He said, "I just don't hear anything that outstanding." To this day Kyle remembers, with regret, his decision.

At the time I was producing Clint, his album went platinum. I was also producing Charlie Daniels when his album went gold. Then along came Tracy Lawrence, and Doug Stone had a platinum album. I was too busy producing acts to have any time left over for A&R responsibilities.

Giant

In 1992, Irving Azoff, the head of Giant Records, approached me to see if I would be interested in opening a division of Giant Records in Nashville. Giant Records is a joint venture entertainment industry owned by Azoff and Time/Warner. Giant headquarters operated out of Los Angeles. I remained at Giant until 1997.

DreamWorks

Mo and Michael Ostin originally approached me about coming to work for DreamWorks. Mo Ostin is head of the music division for DreamWorks Records in Los Angeles. Previously he was president of Warner Bros. Music, Los Angeles, for over twenty years. Mo is thought of as one of the greatest label executives in the history of the music industry. I knew what kind of a reputation Mo had and I knew that DreamWorks was fast becoming the most respected label in the industry. So when Mo asked me to join the company, I was thrilled and honored to join.

Since DreamWorks employees function without titles, I am designated as a principle executive or as president of the Nashville division for

DreamWorks. There is structure within the company insofar as work criteria are concerned; however, titles are not designated per se.

We do have departments and department heads at the label. I am the head of the A&R department and work with one other person, Allison Brown. Johnny Rose is head of our marketing and sales department; our promotion department is headed by Scott Borchetta; and our general manager, who is also in charge of business affairs and administration, is Wayne Halper.

The Movies

I work with Spielberg, Katzenberg, and Geffen, the owners of Dream-Works. We worked on the music for *The Prince Of Egypt*, which came out in 1998. I've only known Steven Spielberg since I joined the company. I flew to California, and we all had a meeting. Working with people of such genius and vision is a dream come true. *Deep Impact, Saving Private Ryan,* and *Mousehunt* have all been astronomically successful, as has every project undertaken with Spielberg at the helm.

Internal Works

The A&R departments are the creative organs of a label. They are responsible for screening and casting songs for the label's artists, signing artists, developing artists, properly casting the creative sides of an artist's project, overseeing the budget, overseeing the entire project to its end, and then passing the finished product along for complete label approval.

Promotion departments deal with the radio media. They promote the artist's product, the singles and the albums, to *Billboard* and *R&R* radio reporting stations.

Publicity departments deal with each and every artist on the label. They also deal with the internal staffs in the various departments of the label, determining what the needs are and taking care of the publicity for the departments. The publicity departments also make sure that the label is well known by keeping the label's name in front of the public and by making sure that positive articles are being produced and read concerning the label's artists and projects. Publicity departments have a very important job because they create the link between the labels and the public from the label's point of view.

The publishing branch of a label is a vital part because the publishing department links our artists with the songs they need to record. Of course, right along with the publishing departments are our staff writers, who write the songs for our recording artists if and when our recording artists are not songwriters or want to listen to other material for their album projects, as is usually the case. The publishing departments also provide the music and lyrics for soundtracks for motion pictures and other music entities, such as videos.

Producers are the liaisons between the artist, the artist's project, and the label executives. The producer oversees the song selection, the artist's budget for the project, and the creative decisions as to what songs will be recorded and what songs will not be recorded for that particular project. The producer is also responsible for casting the session musicians, the studio engineers, the studio, the extra recording equipment, cartage, background vocals, and so on. Lastly, the producer is responsible for the finished product and turning it in to the label for approval.

Departments are definitely interlinked, especially at DreamWorks, because of the way we are structured. Everyone has input and is aware of each other's departments and what they're doing. It makes it more productive and effective for the entire label if each department has an understanding of what the other departments are doing. At our label, we make sure that communication between the departments is up-to-date; therefore, we rarely have conflicts between our departments.

Every one of our individual departments is of equal importance to the label. We try to let everyone have input into every facet of the label's function, whether that function is of a creative or an administrative origin. Everyone's opinion counts equally in making decisions as to the direction and the focus of the label.

DreamWorks is a U.S.-owned company. However, I believe that the labels in Nashville that are foreign owned are not affected by their home offices as far as the creative end of the business is concerned. Nashville labels have become so successful that the corporate offices, wherever they may be located, are allowing the labels to continue doing whatever they are doing in order to stay as successful as they are.

The Artists

Recording artists are brought to the attention of label executives through various means: word of mouth, showcasing, management, and demo tapes. Our company will not sign an artist even if that artist has great talent if he seems to have a bad attitude. An artist can learn how to write, learn to be more proficient on an instrument, and improve his vocal range, but a bad attitude is too hard to deal with and impossible to fix. There are too many wonderfully talented people out there who don't have bad attitudes to choose from. We don't have to put up with huge egos or too many demands from an aspiring artist.

Every artist's contract is different; therefore, the money is divided between the artist, producer, and so on, by virtue of their individual contract. There is no set percentage or set amount designated in contracts—everything is open to negotiations. We may give the artist an advance when their record is completed. We may advance the artist when they sign with the company. Advances have many variables, depending on how successful the individual artist is and on what rung of the ladder they are standing. Of course, we advance more for an established act than we do for a new act.

Currently, DreamWorks has seven artists signed to the company: Randy Travis, Linda Davis, Lisa Angel, Redmond and Vale, Darryl Worley, Jessica Andrews, and Mac McAnally. We look for artists who are unique. We want someone who is a media entertainer because the music always comes first; therefore, the singing part of the artist is our first consideration. But we consider many more aspects today when signing an artist than was the case in Nashville some years ago. Because the business is so huge with worldwide formats, we try to find artists who incorporate many talents: singing ability, writing ability, performing ability, media/video appeal, entertainment value, and youth are big parts of signing artists. Having well-defined social skills is very important. We don't want our artists to have difficulty during live interviews. They need to be confident and articulate.

Being young is important because it takes several years to break an artist and because of the physical and emotional demands of being out on the road. If someone says that age makes no difference, that simply is not true. Labels want to get their investment back and need for the artist to be around for years to come. Record buyers are, for the most part, young, and they want to identify with and view young, good-looking artists who they feel are in touch with their age-group and their feelings.

There needs to be movement in the industry. If all of the older artists were still on labels, there would be no room for the young, talented artists coming along. There are only a few artists who are as viable today as they were at their peak. Randy Travis is one of those few.

Randy Travis

We opened the doors of DreamWorks/Nashville with Randy Travis as our first signed artist. In 1998, the first year we were opened, his record went to number 1 on the *Billboard* charts. You can't do any better than number 1.

I had planned to open our doors with someone like Randy because I knew we needed someone who had instant credibility. We needed an artist who was established and respected enough to be on Letterman, Leno, Rosie O' Donnell, and Regis and Kathie Lee. As soon as those people were contacted, they all wanted Randy to be on their shows. Randy has always had tremendous media and television appeal. I knew that a new artist could never give us this instant recognition. Also, Randy is very intelligent and verbally sophisticated. He handles himself extremely well in media situations, whether they are live or taped. Randy and I have known each other for a long time. I knew what kind of man he is, and I was aware of his great talent.

Growth

The music industry has grown to huge proportions in the last eight to ten years, which has provided Nashville with a great success story and the influx of a lot of money. Many job opportunities have become available because of the success of the music industry. There has been a great deal of growth, not only within the industry but also for the entire city. Also, a good deal of positive attention has been afforded to Nashville as well as Nashville's major labels and their artists.

At times in the past few years, there has been some complacency with our success. We must remember that hard work and creatively working together as a unit is what got us to where we are today. If we don't pay attention to the creative process along with marketing and sales, we could go back to where we were, which is way down the ladder, as far as the music market, record sales, and the number of fans are concerned.

As in any other big-business concern, working at or for a major label boils down to the same criteria used to measure job security in any other market. Money must be made for the corporation and for the community. People must take their jobs seriously and continue to keep up high standards creatively, or else there will be failure. This holds true in any profession.

The process of decision making at DreamWorks involves listening to the opinion of every individual and every designated committee to arrive at a decision. However, the final decisions regarding signing artists, selecting songs, and so on come down to me.

I don't believe that any one person at a major label should have too much control or power. Success testifies to the fact that high standards are kept in place regarding creative and administrative decisions, and it is these high standards that continue to define our success. If our industry were run autocratically, I do not believe we would be successful.

Independent producers are contracted by the label to perform a service that is similar to what an in-house producer does. The money paid to in-house or independent producers is in the same ballpark.

In Nashville, the music industry is extremely competitive but in a very friendly way. The major labels in Nashville are some of the most cooperative entities in the music industry. I don't think Nashville's music indus-

try would have grown as it has if the labels were competitive in a negative way.

Radio

Radio works hand in hand with the labels. Success depends on many
things, and radio is very helpful to the labels by listening to our ideas and
giving us feedback on what the fans want to hear.

Although airplay is critical to the music industry, the number of units
sold is far more important to the label. Units sold means you are receiving
airplay. Units sold means you are selling concert tickets. Units sold means
your product is being accepted by the record-buying and ticket-buying
public. Units sold is the criterion that determines the success or failure of
the artist.

The singles that receive airplay are chosen by various means. Sometimes
we use market analyses and research, combined with going by our gut
feeling. Some artists, while on the road at various predetermined venues,
may try out their songs on live audiences in order to analyze response to
new material. After all the marketing research is in, we will select singles
by considering all of the factors mentioned above.

The Writers

If we have an artist who is also a writer, we will pick songs that the artist
has written or cowritten for the project. Although DreamWorks is a rela-
tively new company in Nashville, DreamWorks writers in California have
been working hard writing scores and lyrics for Spielberg's numerous hit
movies. We also tap our California resources for our Nashville artists.

If an artist is not a writer, we involve all of our departments in defining
that artist. Then we go to the publishing community and explain to them
the focus we have for a certain artist. We stay in touch with the top publishers in the industry. We want their writers to know who our artists are
and what kind of material we are looking for concerning each individual
artist. We talk to writers and publishers about our marketing plans and
direction for that artist. We even have a meeting whereby they can meet
with the artist and hear some of the artist's previously recorded material.
We may ask publishers and writers to look for appropriate songs in their
catalogs, or we may ask them to write new songs. It all depends on what
we are looking for at that specific time for that specific artist. We select
songs for our artists from a wide range of material both inside and outside
of the label.

I'm not into developing writers because if you sign a writer who is not
established and who does not yet know the lay of the land, so to speak, he

may learn and develop at your company while being paid a draw for three years and then may leave thinking there are greener pastures. I'd rather sign writers who have been around and are proven professionals. Of course, I pay a higher draw for veteran writers, but they're worth it. And the chances of them leaving the company are much slimmer because they already know what is out there.

In a staff publishing situation, the writers and the publishers are partners. They split mechanical monies. The starting draw for a writer is usually between $12,000 and $14,000 annually. The sky is the limit for writers who have had great successes. A writer's draws are recouped by the publishing company by deducting monies from the writer's airplay and/or mechanical checks prior to distribution to the writer. Draws are monies paid in advance to the writer, to be recouped by the publishing companies as the writer's royalty monies accrue.

Writers and staff publishers split mechanical monies on a fifty-fifty basis between them. Our label owns active publishing companies, as do all major publishers, with BMI and SESAC, in order to accommodate writers and artist/writers who belong to those performing-rights affiliations.

Our in-house writers are hired by our publishing company. We want to make sure that publishing is healthy at our label. We want to make sure that publishing is a part of our label because it gives us a supply of great songs by great writers. However, we look for and listen to songs from other publishing companies. Our goal is to find the very best songs for our artists.

Goals

In the short term, I want to get our staff used to each other and used to the ins and outs of the music industry. I also want to build up our artist roster as well as our catalog of songs. Randy was our opening act, and we also have Linda Davis on board. Along with the *Prince of Egypt* soundtrack and its country and urban tie-in albums, we will begin to release some projects on some of our new artists. In the long term, DreamWorks wants to become a complete entertainment company. And, because of the support we have with Spielberg, Katzenberg, and Geffen, there are literally no limits as to what we can take on. DreamWorks is based on a standard of creative quality not to be outdone anywhere else in the industry.

If I Could Change Things

If I could make changes in the music industry, I would make the creative aspect of music the most important part of our business. The music is what the bottom line is all about. And, sometimes we, as a business, get side-tracked and blinded by trends and fear. Then paranoia may creep in, and when people get scared creativity may become a bit blurred to other factors. Our industry needs to keep in mind that "music business" is two words and that "music" comes before "business."

I also wish we could do our business without such huge expenditures. I would like to see a way in which we could get to our record buyers, our ticket buyers, and music fans without having to expend the enormous sums of money demanded for advertising and promotion. We are getting to that critical junction where music may be sacrificed for money.

I think when our music gets diluted, rather than staying distinctive, new, and fresh, the country music buyers will demand change by going elsewhere for their entertainment needs. At that point, we will have to say, "If we are going to keep our country fans, then we are going to have to stay fresh and creative." We got to where we are by being creative. We did not get here by spending huge sums of money in marketing plans. The great music got us here. The listeners don't care about marketing plans. The fans care about great music and great artists. If we don't continue to furnish these products, we're back to where we were in 1988, when we were selling very few records and the country market was very small and unpopular outside of Nashville.

We've been very blessed for the last several years because of the great artists like Randy Travis, Clint Black, Garth Brooks, and Alan Jackson. These great artists, along with their great music, helped the country music business become a huge international business.

We now have a worldwide fan base. These fans expect to hear unique and creative music. However, because the Nashville music community is small and close-knit, at times there is a tendency to follow the leader rather than attempting to be creative, fresh, and unique. If we don't stretch our creative minds and make efforts to be different, we will eventually lose all the business we have built up over the last few years. We cannot afford to go backward. We have too broad a base.

As a final thought, I'd like to reiterate that there is no better place to work in the area of music than Nashville, Tennessee. I have a saying: "You either make dust or eat dust." If you're good enough, strong enough, tough enough, and creative enough, you will do well. If you're not totally committed to music in all the areas I just mentioned, then you better stay out of the way because you will get run over.

2

Danny Kee

Reprise and Warner Bros. Records

There's place and means for every man alive.

—William Shakespeare

About Reprise Records

Reprise was established by Frank Sinatra but lay dormant for years until Warner Bros. revived it in 1986 with the issue of Dwight Yoakam's first album. Sinatra founded Reprise in 1961, after he grew angry with Capitol Records. Capitol refused to allow Sinatra his own personal label, and it declined to raise his royalty rate above 5 percent, considered standard at the time. But Sinatra's contract with Capitol allowed him to record an album for another label for each album he turned in to Capitol.

Sinatra had wanted to buy Verve Records, one of the major labels in jazz, but Sinatra's lawyer also represented Norman Granz, the head of Verve. The lawyer sold Verve to MGM for more than Sinatra could buck up but stole the key players from Verve to help Sinatra establish Reprise.

Sinatra was notorious for his hatred of rock 'n roll. Even though it was the growing music medium in the nation, Sinatra insisted on a roster of artists who clearly had hit their stride in another era: Dean Martin, Sammy Davis Jr., Keely Smith, Dinah Shore, Dennis Day, Rosemary Clooney—in all, more than 100 acts. Sinatra himself was the key moneymaker, but, because half of his material was coming out on Capitol, he wasn't generating nearly enough to keep the label in the black.

When it became clear Reprise wasn't cutting it, Sinatra finally gave in and hired Jimmy Bowen, who had dabbled in numerous parts of the record business, to head the A&R department and find some younger acts. Bowen realized quickly that the roster was too large and too unprofitable, and he convinced Sinatra that about eighty acts would have to be trimmed.

In the meantime, Warner Bros. wanted Sinatra's services as an actor and made a deal in September 1963 to purchase Reprise for $1.5 million. In addition, Sinatra would receive a one-third interest in Warners.

Bowen managed to revive several of the Reprise careers: Dean Martin earned a hit in 1964 with Bowen producing "Everybody Loves Somebody," while Sinatra garnered Top 5 records in 1966 with "Strangers in the

14

Night" and "That's Life," particularly impressive considering that the Beatles and Motown dominated the musical scene at the time. Bowen also brought Kenny Rogers and the First Edition, while through other sources the label acquired the services of Joni Mitchell and Neil Young.

Reprise eventually fell dormant in the Warner vaults, although there was a light at the tunnel's end. Dwight Yoakam, a left-of-center country artist from Los Angeles, emerged with Warner Bros. in 1986, hitting with his very first single, a remake of Johnny Horton's "Honky Tonk Man." Yoakam was placed on a renewed Reprise label, and he brought a certain respect immediately to the Reprise name. Yoakam hasn't always been a darling of country radio, but he has established critical respect for his willingness to experiment with a variety of genres while always keeping that hillbilly twang in the music.

During the mid-1990s, Nashville record labels went through a period of expansion, most of them establishing sister labels that would give them more muscle in the marketplace. But because nearly every label followed suit, the approach merely increased the cost of marketing, while the outlets available for the surplus labels and surplus artists did not increase. In many cases, particularly in radio, the opportunities actually decreased.

During this period, Reprise worked primarily as a second logo, though Warner Bros. employees continued to work the records. Warner considered establishing Reprise as a stand-alone label, but in the end the label wisely decided not to pull the trigger. Instead, it established a shared promotion department with Giant Records, one of the other small labels in the WEA (Warner/Elektra/Atlantic) family. Two label chiefs were established for Warner and Reprise: Bob Saporiti at Warner Bros., and Bill Mayne at Reprise. Both report to Warner Bros. president Jim Ed Norman.

Michael Peterson found success on the Reprise label under that set up, emerging in 1997 with "Drink, Swear, Steal and Lie" and gaining one of the top-selling debut albums of the year. Reprise has also been renewed on the pop side, with Chris Isaak and Take-6, signed through the Nashville office, emerging on the label.

About Warner Bros.

It is appropriate that Warner Bros. Records is a major player in the country music field, because Warner Bros. has a significant place in the history of recorded sound. During the early years of the film industry, Hollywood was skeptical of early developments that would combine moving pictures with sound. Only a handful of moguls felt that the public would buy into such a mix. Four of those moguls were Warner brothers: Samuel, Harry, Albert, and Jack, who formed the Vitaphone Company for the express purpose of developing the concept.

Vitaphone gave its first public display at the Warner Bros. Theater in New York on August 6, 1926, featuring several short subjects plus a silent movie, *Don Juan,* starring John Barrymore, which included some sound effects. On October 6, 1927, the Warners presented *The Jazz Singer* in New York, with Al Jolson, and the movies were forever altered.

Still it would take more than three decades before Warner Bros. expanded from the movies into the record business. The company established its home in Burbank, California, during 1960 and made a commitment to the industry by signing the Everly Brothers to one of the first million-dollar contracts stretching over ten years. The Everlys immediately rewarded the firm with its first number 1 record, "Cathy's Clown."

Warner did not open a country branch at that time, although the company did find quick success in the genre, as Bob Luman scored a Top 10 single with "Let's Think About Living" by the end of 1960. Warner would not have another country hit for thirteen years.

In 1971, the label made very open overtures to Nashville, confirming in a front-page story in *Billboard* that they intended to open a Nashville office. And though country music is an American art form, it was an Englishman, former Rolling Stones publicist Andy Wickham, who led the charge for a Nashville Warner wing. Brought to Warner as an A&R executive in 1966, Wickham helped form a bridge between the Burbank label and the Music City establishment. Warner Bros. met many of the movers and shakers in early-1970s Nashville and recognized a skepticism about new labels. Warner realized that it would require a huge financial commitment to make it work.

It didn't hurt when the label reaped an unexpected country hit in 1973. "Dueling Banjos," a remake of a 1955 song called "Feudin' Banjos" fashioned by Eric Weissberg and Steve Mandell for the movie *Deliverance,* went all the way to number 5 on the country chart. By the end of the year, Warner had hired Memphis record producer Chips Moman to oversee A&R for the fledgling Nashville office. Moman had developed impressive credentials in pop music, with a hand in such hits as the Box Tops' "The Letter," Elvis Presley's "In the Ghetto" and "Suspicious Minds," Dusty Springfield's "Son of a Preacher Man," and B. J. Thomas's "Hooked on a Feeling."

In 1974 Warner sent six singles into the country charts, and in 1975 the company finally established a hit with an artist who was something more than a mere novelty. Emmylou Harris reached the Top 5 with "If I Could Only Win Your Love," an old Louvin Brothers tune. Harris would become the first artist of significance on Warner and would set the tone for the label with her penchant for diversity. She would record a bluegrass/country/rock album along with Dolly Parton and Linda Ronstadt, and eventually she recorded music with an alternative edge.

Warner's early years were just as diverse. The company signed Donna Fargo, who had crossed numerous hits from country to pop, and added well-established country figure Buck Owens, who had been making hits for fifteen years. They added Margo Smith, who excelled in country remakes of pop hits; Rex Allen Jr., whose father had been an important figure in western music; and Gary Morris, who worked in everything from country/rock to opera. And Warner signed John Anderson, whose traditional voice was often compared to the late Lefty Frizzell. In 1983, Anderson scored the first million-selling single for Warner Bros., "Swingin'."

Moman, whose business acumen wasn't nearly as strong as his creative mind, departed Warner before any of that came to be. Norro Wilson, who had written such hits as Charlie Rich's "The Most Beautiful Girl," Joe Stampley's "Soul Song," and George Jones's "The Grand Tour," headed the Warner Bros. for four years. In June 1980, the label turned to Frank Jones, who had worked alongside Columbia Records executive Don Law during the 1960s.

In early 1983, Warner Bros. merged with Elektra/Asylum, and the Warner staff was dismissed in favor of the Elektra/Asylum team assembled by Jimmy Bowen, the controversial producer who had come to Nashville in the mid-1970s after producing the likes of Frank Sinatra and Dean Martin in Los Angeles. Bowen had made Warner Bros. one of the most successful labels in Nashville, with Conway Twitty, Hank Williams Jr., Crystal Gayle, Eddie Rabbitt, and the Bellamy Brothers. Added to a roster that already included John Anderson, Gary Morris, T. G. Sheppard, Emmylou Harris, David Frizzell and Shelly West, Warner Bros. instantly became a massive country presence.

At the time, Bowen had already negotiated to bring Los Angeles producer Jim Ed Norman into the fold at Elektra. Norman, who had moved to Los Angeles as a member of Shiloh, which included Eagle-to-be Don Henley, had a hit the very first time he produced a record, Jennifer Warnes's "It's the Right Time of the Night," in 1977. Just three years later, he was one of the hottest production figures in the business, thanks in part to the movie *Urban Cowboy*, for which he produced Mickey Gilley's "Stand by Me" and Anne Murray's "Could I Have This Dance." Norman also produced Johnny Lee's smooth follow-ups to "Lookin' for Love."

When the merger occurred, Norman's contract was transferred to Warner Bros. and, though he had never before worked at a record company, he came to Nashville as the label's head of A&R. By the next year, when Bowen left Warner to run MCA (Music Corporation of America) Records, Norman was the new Warner Bros. chief.

Again, diversity was a key element under Norman's vision for Warner Bros. The company formed a progressive department, through which it signed the likes of pop singer/songwriter Beth Nielsen Chapman and banjo-led jazz act Bela Fleck and the Flecktones. The company established a Warner Western label and branched out into Christian music as well.

More important, while Norman had established his reputation by making easy-listening country as a producer, he felt that a certain edge had been lacking in country music. He added Randy Travis to Warner and Dwight Yoakam to the Reprise label, and Warner Bros. became a leading force in the New Traditionalist movement of the late 1980s, which embodied traditional country music with an edge.

Warner Bros. has established a reputation as an unusual label in Nashville. The company is willing to go against the grain, signing country/rock-influenced Travis Tritt in the middle of the New Traditionalist era, taking a chance on the Forester Sisters when multi-female acts didn't exist, and more recently signing Grand Ole Opry stars Bill Anderson and Connie Smith at a time when labels routinely view acts over the age of thirty as too old.

The Warner staff is decidedly relaxed and is often more open to unusual ideas than some of the other labels in town. That isn't necessarily reflected in its home, however. The Warner building, dedicated in 1994, is a large, imposing complex made of stone, and visitors have to climb to the second floor before they can even see a receptionist. Entry to the building requires gaining permission from a security officer with a sawed-off shotgun.

Danny Kee

Growing Up

I was born on the southwest side of Chicago on March 26, 1963. I was raised in the suburbs with my younger sister, Kristin. Both of my parents were teachers. My mother, Shirley, taught grade school, and my dad, Byron, taught industrial arts at the college level. Eventually, my dad and mom moved to Mansfield, Ohio, which is located between Columbus and Cleveland. My dad was promoted from teaching to dean and later became president of North Central Technical College in Mansfield. This move took place after I had left home to begin college.

Although I was too young to remember, I've been told that I first showed an interest in music when my father came to my crib in the wee hours of the night to tend to me. My dad was a fan of big-band music, and he would turn on the music as he took care of my needs when I was just an infant. I've been told that I really liked the music; it had a wonderful soothing effect on me, and I would go back to sleep when dad played it.

As I grew older, I continued to interact with my dad in a positive way when he played his favorite music. When I began to walk and talk I would ask that music be played for me, and at times I would go over to the radio and try to find the right station so I could listen to the wonderful sounds emanating from the speakers.

Both of my parents were supportive of me in my musical pursuits. I, like many children, took the dreaded piano lessons, which I didn't really appreciate. I was not interested in being a piano player. I didn't like to practice, and because of my lack of interest, my attention span was not conducive to thoroughly learning the piano. However, I was introduced to music through these lessons and decided that I wanted to be a drummer. My parents made a deal with me that if I would continue my piano lessons for one year, which to a fourth-grader seemed like an eternity, they would buy me a set of drums; I agreed. I got my first set of drums when I was ten years old, and I drove everybody crazy banging away on those drums. My parents were very patient and tolerant.

19

I taught myself most of the drum licks. I'd listen to all the records I could get my hands on and focused on the sounds of the drums. The Beatles were very influential in my musical repertoire, as were the Rolling Stones. I also really liked the drummer who played for the rock group Rush at that time. I listened over and over and taught myself how to play the riffs and licks of those great drummers.

The formalized learning I undertook was very rudimental. It was limited to the snare drum for the marching band in which I played in junior high and high school. I also performed at solo contests, and I actually took a first place at the State of Illinois Solo Contest when I was thirteen years old.

Like many other teenagers who had a great interest in music, I eventually put a band together, and we played at shopping malls and private parties and in garages. At that time, I felt that the drums were played in a very low key and basic way and that the guitar and bass players had a lot more creative leeway than did the drummers; they had so much more music as opposed to just the rhythm involved in playing the drums. So, for these reasons and because a guitar was a whole lot easier to take from place to place than were a full set of drums, I began to learn to play guitar.

Education

As I mentioned earlier, I went off to college when mom and dad moved to Mansfield. I entered Illinois State University as a business major, but I continued playing guitar all through college. Although being a great session musician has never been my main aspiration, I love playing and creating music.

Because no one in my family had a background in music, it had not yet dawned on me that I could have a career in the music industry. I grew up with the understanding that if I ever wanted to earn a decent living, I would have to get a degree in business and that, unless I wanted to live in poverty, I should not major in music or art. My parents wanted more for me than they had had, so they both encouraged me to get a business degree.

When I was a junior, I had gone through many dull business courses, accounting courses, law, economics, and so on. I still wanted to do something in the music industry, so I decided that I would finish my business degree but that I was also going to pursue music.

Although Illinois State is a very fine university, its music department is not its main thrust. However, it did have an ensemble class there, and I began to get involved working with the ensemble. Illinois State didn't offer any contemporary music courses, nor did the university offer any courses in music business. If you happened to be a music major at Illinois State, you would be confined to playing your instrument without having any supportive courses except for classical music theory and classical composition.

I began to realize that since there were record companies and recording artists on MTV, there must be a university that offered courses in the music business. I began to research the industry at the library. I read *Billboard* and all other sources that applied to the professional music industry. I also obtained a national university directory and began to write to various institutions of higher learning inquiring as to what type of courses and curriculum they offered specifically geared to working in the music industry. Of the many responses I received, it seemed to me that colleges on the West Coast offered the courses I would be most interested in. I presented my findings to my parents, and again they were very supportive of me in my desire to find a college geared to the courses I wanted to pursue. I have been blessed with great parents, and I am grateful to them for always being there for me.

Although my parents didn't know anything about the professional music business and had no personal interest in it, they encouraged me to follow my dreams. All they asked was that I finish my education in business before pursuing the music business. I finished my courses in business and got my bachelors degree from Illinois State.

In 1985, soon after graduating, I left for the West Coast. My plan was to enroll in UCLA's night program, which offered music business courses. It also had notable people employed in the music industry teach some of the classes. Other than wanting to enter UCLA, I didn't have my life very well planned, especially financially. I arrived in California with less than $500 in my wallet, driving an old, beat-up car. Eventually, I realized that I had to regroup, so I moved back home, tended bar, and saved some money.

Moving to Nashville

I made more inquiries into the music business, this time concentrating on colleges around the Nashville area. Once again, employing the use of the national college directory, I wrote to Belmont College and MTSU (Middle Tennessee State University). I was very impressed with the responses I received from those institutions.

When I had saved some money and was sure my car would make it, I drove to Nashville to check out the area and the colleges. Since I already had my undergraduate degree, I was not interested in seeking another degree, especially since, for the most part, degrees are meaningless in the music industry. Therefore, I enrolled in classes that I felt would be of the greatest benefit to me in my pursuit of obtaining employment in the industry.

I was on my own, and I learned as much as I could about the business. Internships were part of the university curriculum wherein you worked approximately ten hours a week in a business while taking other classes. I took courses at MTSU in the spring, summer, and fall of 1986. In 1987, I secured an internship in the A&R department at Warner Bros. Records.

It was extremely difficult to get that internship. Of all the information I had garnered about the music business throughout my college years, and doing research on my own, the most valuable piece of information I learned was that employment in the music business is highly sought after and unbelievably competitive. The professors and the teachers at MTSU drilled it into our heads that each year, in the Nashville music business, there were only twenty or twenty-five available placements for students and that there were somewhere between 300 and 350 graduates with degrees in music business coming out of Nashville area colleges and universities.

I took their advice seriously and knew I would have to be innovative and assertive and have great tenacity in order to be placed and to hang onto any job I might be fortunate enough to come by in the music industry. There was a line of students applying for internships at Warner Bros. Records that went from the entrance door, down the street, and around the block. They were all willing to work without pay just to get inside the door.

Getting in the Door at Warner Bros. Records

When I was fortunate enough to get my internship at Warner Bros.— thanks to Martha Sharp, Paige Levy, and Barry Beckett, who were working in Warner's A&R department at that time—I decided that instead of taking classes and work at my internship at the same time, I would finish all of my course work and devote all of my time to my internship. Instead of working just ten hours a week, I decided to come to work at 9:00 A.M. with all the other Warner Bros. employees. I didn't leave until almost everyone else had left for the day. Eventually, I became a permanent fixture at Warner Bros. I decided that I wasn't going to leave until they gave me full-time employment.

I literally did everything and anything for anyone who needed something done. I copied tapes, called on publishers, answered the phones (including answering the phones at the front desk), screened songs, worked in the mail room, ran errands, got their lunches, and made the coffee. I did everything I could humanly do with a genuine smile on my face. I never forgot how prized the position was that I was inhabiting.

My internships ran consecutively from the spring through the summer, and I was determined to be employed at the label when my internships had ended. I wanted the people I worked for at the label to feel so bad about my leaving that they would offer me a job.

In my last month, I kept hinting around that I was going to have to leave soon and I was looking for work. But nobody offered me a job. I began to get a bit nervous; I decided to take a proactive approach. I decided to walk in and talk to the president of the company, Jim Ed Norman. I'd just tell him that I've been a good intern and I just want a job and that I'd do anything he felt I could do.

Cindy Finch, who is currently vice president of administration for Warner Bros., was at that time Jim Ed's assistant. Cindy's desk was directly outside of Jim Ed's closed office door. Cindy was very good at her job. She was in charge of his schedule and knew he had barely enough time to fulfill the daily demands made on him, let alone talk to a pesky intern. But Jim Ed was always very open and nice to me whenever we passed each other in the hallways. So I waited until Cindy was away from her post to peek into Jim Ed's office. Fortunately, that day his door was not closed. I could hear him finishing up a phone call, so I waited until I heard him hang up the receiver. Then I tapped on his door and meekly said, "May I speak with you for a moment?"

He was really nice. He got up from his desk and came around and said, "Sure, come on in," as he shook my hand. I said, "I'm an intern here in the A&R department." He said, "Oh yeah, I know who you are." (I thought to myself, "You dummy. Of course he knows who you are—you've been hanging around every day, ten to twelve hours a day for six months.")

Since I still didn't think that I had really been noticed by the president, I told him about all of the things I had done during my internship and that I just wanted to work at Warner Bros. I said that Warner Bros. was the best label and had the best recording artists and the best staff of people, that I just really wanted to work here, and even though I wasn't getting paid, that this was the best job I'd ever had. I continued to tell him I'd continue to answer phones, do mail room work—whatever he wanted done, I would gladly do it, including working as the janitor, if I could just work at Warner Bros. Record.

Well, we had a great discussion, but finally Jim Ed said, "We really aren't hiring anybody right now, but, of course, I will keep you in mind should there be an opening." About three weeks after our meeting, I was really shaking in my shoes thinking I had no chance of working at the label I had grown to feel I had become a part of. I was into my last week. Most of the friends I had made in Nashville were working at record stores because they couldn't get a job at a label. I had spent what savings I had. I'd moved far from home. Now what? I was feeling pretty down.

Then my phone rings, and it's Jim Ed Norman. He says, "I'm really busy producing nine recording artists' albums every year, including Crystal Gayle, Kenny Rogers, Michael Martin Murphey, Mac McAnally, the Forester Sisters, and so on. This is a lot for me to contend with and I could use some help. So I was wondering if you would be interested in working directly for me as my production assistant. And since you previously mentioned to me that you are interested in producing artists, I will teach what I know about producing records."

Well, I had to think about my answer for about one millionth of a second. I said, "Absolutely. Of course. Consider me there." And I began to work at Warner Bros. Records in the fall of 1987.

For my first four years at the label, I followed Jim Ed around, worked with him in all the various studios, listened to everything he did, and helped him screen songs and put songs on hold for various artists. After about two years, publishers and songwriters who couldn't get in to see Jim Ed began bringing me their songs. They'd call me and ask if I would listen. I didn't feel as though I was qualified to screen songs on my own, but I began to listen to songs and meet with writers and publishers. Eventually, I began to call on the publishers and writers I had met and tell them when we were looking for songs for particular recording artists. I began to bring some of the songs I thought were particularly outstanding to Jim Ed to listen to.

Jim Ed was always very gracious when I brought him songs to listen to. But a long time passed before he finally thought I had picked a winner for the project. One day he said, "Let me play that one for Kenny or Crystal."

Then another considerable amount of time went by as I continued to evolve into a real A&R person with a discerning understanding of what song was best for what artist and finally began to get some of the songs I had brought to Jim Ed recorded by our artists.

To this day, I still don't know how anyone ever gets a job at a record label. I've never seen an ad in the paper reading "Salary negotiable. Apply at Warner Bros. Records." All jobs in the industry are handled through the inside of the industry, word of mouth, connections through college internships, and so on. I still feel fortunate that I got my job at Warner Bros. when I did. I had just gotten out of college and I had no family or responsibility other than to myself, so I was able to focus totally on working at the label. In 1998, I will have been here for ten years. It's the only job I've ever had other than delivering pizza and being a bartender.

I'm sure that everyone who works in our industry has their story to tell about how they got their first break. I am also sure that no two stories are alike.

Inside Reprise

Our home office is in Burbank, California. My boss, Jim Ed Norman, is the president of the Nashville division of Reprise. He answers to the chairman of the board, Russ Thyret. The Burbank president of Warner Bros. is affectionately referred to as Phil Q [Quartararo].

Time Warner owns the Warner Music Group, which consists of all the record companies: Warner Bros. Records, Reprise Records, Atlantic Records, Asylum Records, and Elektra Records. The Warner Music Group also owns the publishing branch, Warner/Chappell Publishing Company. WEA (Warner/Elektra/Atlantic) is our distribution company. WEA is also owned by Time Warner and is part of the Warner Music Group. WEA distributes for all of the previously named record companies.

I've never worked at any other companies so I can only speak for Reprise Records. Warner/Reprise/Nashville is broken down into Warner Bros. Records and Reprise Records. Each label has its own artists' roster. Also, there are employees at our company who specifically work for either Reprise or Warner Bros.; however, some departments work for both labels.

There is a great deal that goes into a project from its inception to its completion and from the selection of the material to the recording of the project and all the way through to the artwork designs and the final packaging of the product. Our company has three people in the A&R department, and Jim Ed works closely with the A&R staff.

Warner's A&R department is not specific to either Reprise or Warner Bros. Records. We seek out new artists to sign to one of our two labels and listen to tapes of songs for artists already signed to our labels. Lately, I've been spending a considerable amount of time looking for new material for Faith Hill and for a new artist, Anita Cochran. Anita recently had a number 1 record doing a duet with Steve Wariner. Finding our successful artists new material is very high on my priority list.

A&R functions as the creative musical department within the company. We interface with all of our other departments because, in addition to finding songs, finding artists, and helping artists find their way through the system, we also help artists develop relationships with record producers, publishers, writers, and so on. If you think of the departments at our label as an assembly line, A&R would be the first job on the line. We are in charge of putting the music together and making an album. Once we have the music together, then we brainstorm and have meetings with our publicity and promotion departments to develop ideas about how we are going to take this music to the marketplace, how we are going to present this music to the public and to radio. We also talk about videos. We decide whether having videos on this project would be an asset. And if they are an asset, we discuss how to make a visual entrance to the marketplace. A lot of time is spent on determining how the videos should be created and produced.

The publicity department is in charge of everything that relates to the press. The publicity department obtains interviews for the artists and written reviews for the project and the artist, mails albums to the appropriate people, and tries to get a buzz stirred up in the media. They also work with television, from Rosie O'Donnell, to Oprah, to David Letterman and Jay Leno. They try to get our artists booked to make appearances on various high-exposure television programs.

We work the music on a per project basis, so I would look at the function of the promotion department as promoting the album, although promotion people also promote the artist. The function of promotion, calling on radio stations, is completely separate and apart from the function of the publicity department. The promotion department is a staff of individuals who have relationships with the various radio programmers. We have six people in our promotion department stationed around the country and one person in our Nashville office coordinating with our other promotion people throughout the United States. These six people divide up all of the *Billboard-* and *R&R* (*Radio & Record*)-reporting radio stations in the entire country. And, from their various regions, they develop relationships with key radio people. They travel to and visit radio stations on their roster on a frequent basis. They do everything within their scope and power that is ethical and legal to get our records played on the radio as opposed to music from other record companies. They also promote our products to *R&R* and *Gavin*. We do not have a separate sales, art, publicity, or A&R staff. The two labels share these departments. But we do have separate marketing and promotion departments.

The marketing department is very small but very important. It is in charge of all ideas and efforts toward taking our products to the marketplace. It interfaces with our publicity, sales, and promotion departments in their marketing efforts. It is basically an idea-generating department that focuses on the best route to take the album to the marketplace.

The A&R department oversees the entire creative process. It interfaces with songwriters, publishers, and producers, and keeps track of recording budgets, the musicians' credits, liner notes, writer and publisher credits, and everything else that is printed in or on the packaging. It also makes sure everybody is compensated correctly. And, once the project is completed, it sends out letters to the publishers and writers and sends out copies of the project thanking the appropriate people.

Two Labels

For a while, Reprise had gained the reputation of being more progressive than its sister label, Warner Bros., because Dwight Yoakam was on Reprise and Randy Travis was on Warner Bros. However, that is really not the case. We have two distinct labels at our company because having two labels gives us more leverage in the marketplace. If you think of radio time as being just so many hours in the day, there is only so much radio time that is afforded to each label; therefore, by having two labels, we receive a greater share of radio time. And radio airplay is the main avenue for selling our product.

When we had a new record coming out, let's say on Randy Travis, our promotion department called the radio stations to try to get the music directors and program directors of those stations to listen to our new record and hopefully add it to their play list. With an artist like Randy Travis, it was obviously easy to get them to add the record, but when you are trying to break new artists, it is a bit more difficult.

At the time we had Randy on our label, we also had Dwight Yoakam, Highway 101, Kenny Rogers, Crystal Gayle, the Forester Sisters, and many more. They were all putting out new albums and new singles, and they all needed to be added to radio play lists. We began to hear from radio that they were not really sure that they could add another artist from the same label. Again, there were only so many slots open for each label.

Not only does competition exist between the labels, but now artists are competing within the same label for airplay. Now we go to radio with two different companies and two different promotion staffs. Other major labels have also formed several in-house labels: RCA has BNA Records and RCA Records; Sony has Columbia, Lucky Dog, Epic, and Monument Records; Curb has Curb Records and MCG/Curb; and MCA has MCA Records and Decca Records. So this approach is not unique to Reprise. All major companies are vying for radio time.

Signing Artists

I will preface my explanation of how artists are signed to major labels by stating that my only experience has been with Reprise Records. I am sure that there are many labels in Nashville and many labels throughout the country that all have different criteria for signing artists. Even at Reprise there have been many different ways that artists have come to be signed to our label.

Faith Hill

I was very involved in the signing of Faith to Reprise. Faith is a unique example. She was working with a songwriter in town named Gary Burr. Gary had kind of taken Faith under his wing, and she would sing with him whenever Gary did writers' nights around town. Although I know Faith has written songs, I don't think she had, at that time, written with Gary.

Along with doing live writers' nights with Gary, Faith also sang on Gary's songwriter's demo, which was pitched around town to various labels and publishers. The demo tape was pitched to me through Maypop Music. Martha Sharp, senior vice president of A&R, became very interested in Faith and thought that she was extremely talented. On several occasions, Martha went out to the Bluebird Cafe to hear and see Faith perform at writers' nights. Gary would always have Faith sing background vocals with him, and once in a while he would let her get up to the mike and sing entire songs as the lead singer.

Eventually, a level of interest and awareness developed at our company about who Faith was—Faith is a very likable, charming person. Every time she would come into the office, everybody would love to see her. So she went through the process and did a lot of demo recording at the Warner Bros. Studio. She continued to sing on more demos with Gary Burr. Eventually, she ended up on television doing a song with Gary. Scott Hendricks, a prominent independent producer in Nashville, just happened to be watching that show. He called and said, "Hey, who is that new artist? I'd really be interested in working with her." So, she met Scott Hendricks, and that's how her first album came into existence.

There are a lot of different ways that artists become signed to the company. Most of the time it involves getting the attention and capturing the admiration of someone in the A&R department or somebody at the record company who listens and says, "Wow! This is really something."

The ante has gone up greatly in the ten short years I've been at the company. I've seen things change considerably in the level of education and the level of being prepared that new artists must have today. The new artists are far more sophisticated today than they once were. Some of the new sophistication has to do with the new technology. New technology has created new ways to do things; for instance, recording at home is a lot easier today than it was just ten years ago. I really feel that the level of talent we now get is just extraordinary compared to what it was five to ten years ago. Some artists who were signed a few years ago would not be signed today. I think it's the same in pro sports. Players who played ten or fifteen years ago may not be able to keep up with the new athletes.

In country music, at least at Warner Bros., it is not only that the talent is far more cultivated but also that the artists are more savvy in terms of understanding the recording business. Artists are coming in today who have already recorded complete albums and who have already obtained a working relationship with management; they have a team in place, they have booking agents, and they've got a whole lot together. Consequently, you now have a record company looking at the artist who has the most going for him, who understands the business, who has a good manager in place, and so on.

When we signed Faith, she didn't have management. She was working at a job in the music business with Reba, and she was working with Gary Burr. She was knowledgeable, and her talent was phenomenal.

Travis Tritt

When Travis first came to our label, he had already gotten to a level with his artistry that was amazing. Travis had it all together. He had been in Atlanta, playing original tunes with his band at Miss Kitty's six nights a week. He was earning his living playing his music. He wasn't working at a day gig and playing music on weekends or as a hobby. He had a lot in place.

Travis's knowledge of the business made signing him far more appealing than most. We wanted to be in business with someone who already had so many pieces of the puzzle put together. He knew who he was artistically, and he had a great deal of business sense.

Talent is a given, but does the artist have savvy, intelligence, and common sense? Can they write songs? Do they have a style that sets them apart from the thousands and thousands of other talented people who are looking for record deals? Travis had everything together. Along with being a great talent, he had a unique style, so he was signed.

How A Deal Works

A spec [speculation] deal is when an artist gets studio engineers and musicians to donate free time to their session with the idea that if the project gets picked up by a label whereby their costs are covered, then they will pay everybody. Everybody who records for us is always paid; we never do anything on a spec deal. We have an agreement with all of the musicians, engineers, studios, background vocalists, and so on that on any project we undertake, we always pay.

Since it is impossible for anyone to predict various intangibles regarding new artists—like how well they write, play an instrument, work in a studio, interpret songs, get along with their producer, and so on—we take things one step at a time. Even though we treat everyone equally, we no longer refer to new artists as "development deals" because some people were offended by the term, thinking that the term gave them a lesser status with the company. Since we give just as much support to new artists as we do to our seasoned artists, we didn't want anyone to feel uncomfortable; so we now refer to new artists as "new artists."

We won't necessarily complete an entire album on a new artist for several reasons. Sometimes we may believe there is a lot of potential but that, given the huge cost of recording today, it wouldn't make sense to turn out completed projects on artists we are not going to pick up on a permanent basis. It can cost as much as $200,000 to complete an album today. We certainly don't want to spend $200,000 to find out that we don't want to make an album with this artist after all. So we'll spend $25,000 or so and cut three or four tunes. This is also much better for the artist because if we are not happy with three or four songs, we can go back into the studio. However, if we have already spent $200,000, it is far less likely we would go back and try again at $200,000 per shot.

If I were an artist, I'd rather go into the studio and cut two or three songs, turn them into the company, and have them say, "Listen, you know I'm not really sure that this came off as well as it can. Why don't you go back into the studio and try again with a different producer or with a different approach with regard to your song material." We are not trying to cut costs as much as we are trying to give our company and our artists as many opportunities as are reasonably feasible.

We are currently working with a female artist who has turned in ten sides and has gone in the studio on three different occasions. We do believe in her. She has demonstrated to us that she has the patience and the intelligence to get the job done, and her album will be released when we know it is right and when we know we can take it to radio with confidence.

Making Music for Money

Artists are not employees of the label. We have a contractual relationship with our artists. We always give an advance to our artists, and as they become more successful the amount of the advance escalates considerably. The motivation in giving a new artist an advance is so they will have some money to live on while they devote their time to making their record. Since there are many things we do with a new artist to prepare them for the professional music business, we must have their undivided attention; therefore, we don't want them to have to get a job to pay their rent or buy groceries.

The advance figures vary, but the range is somewhere between $20,000 and $35,000, depending on the individual artist's circumstances. Typically, we issue half of the advance up front, then we lay down some songs and work with the artist developing his career. We make practice videos to help them become aware of themselves on camera, and we help them to learn the fine technique of giving interviews. Kip Kirby works with our company. She has a professional media school. She teaches artists how to answer questions during an interview. Kip's media school program is very structured and extremely beneficial to our artists.

We also make video demos on our artists. We loosely refer to this process as "video school." We do this because we have had some experiences where an artist will complete a $75,000 video, and the artist will not be happy with it. Our video school enables artists to view themselves and correct anything they don't like about themselves prior to doing the final $75,000 video.

When their record is mixed, completed, accepted by the company, and ready to go, then the artist receives the second half of his advance. Artists are also paid a royalty, which is a fixed percentage of the sale price of their album. Percentages vary from artist to artist on the basis of their level of success. However, contracts today are at times sixty pages long, and there are many factors that may contribute to arriving at the artists' percentage of sales royalty. Every contract is negotiated differently because there are so many factors that are included in artists' contracts.

Producers are also paid a percentage of record sales. Producers also receive half of an advance up front and the rest at completion of their project. Our only in-house producer is Jim Ed; all other producers who work with our artists are hired on an independent basis.

Songwriters and publishers are paid a flat fee on their songs on mechanical payments. ASCAP, BMI, or SESAC pays the publishers and the writers their royalties on airplay.

Changing Times

I am a strong believer in competition being positive. When things get really tight, people get conservative and no one wants to try anything too different. Consequently, some artists begin to sound alike; songs go along with a proven trend, and a lot of sameness happens. Then one day, someone says, "I'll try something different." Things begin to change, and artists come along like Shania Twain. She's incredible.

A successful record person like Jim Ed keeps a lighthearted atmosphere at the company. If someone makes a mistake, they are not ridiculed. I've been very lucky to be at a company where the attitude is so warm and supportive.

Things change rapidly in our industry. There is no real job security in the major music industry. It is extremely rare that someone is with only one company as long as I've been at Warner. I've had extreme stability here. But, by the same token, each day I'm prepared that this may be my last day. People lose their jobs from time to time; nobody is immune to job turnover. The people who take risks are confirmed by the buying public and have what I call synthetic power. You're as secure as your last good call.

In the Hands of a Few

Our business is unique from other large businesses because we are dealing with art. We make art. We are accountable to sell that art to the public. We have to live at the corner of Art and Commerce Streets; and, if our product is not selling, we will not be able to stay in business.

There are various hierarchies of control or power within a label. But if the records are not selling, then whoever had the power no longer has the power any more. For example, if a record company such as Warner Bros. were run by someone who didn't allow other people in the company to have the freedom to make decisions and creative choices, and they absorbed all of the responsibility for making creative choices themselves and dictated those choices to everyone else, there would be nothing to prevent them from doing that. However, they would have to do a pretty darn good job in order to keep that power within their hands, and they had better be selling.

Since we are held accountable to the marketplace to deliver art that is acceptable and commercially viable, I can't imagine any one person who would be able to make decisions and be, across the board, successful in selling art to the varied tastes of a worldwide population.

Our company does not work that way. Everyone in our A&R department has the opportunity to be able to pursue any project they feel might be beneficial to the company. However, people who are working on an individual project are accountable to bring their project in for review. Many times we have gone to the marketplace with a project that not everyone at the label agreed with. However, one or two people at the label were so committed to the project that they weren't going to take no for an answer.

The above scenario actually happened, and the project was extremely successful. When there are experiences like that, the company becomes more flexible about allowing individuals in various departments to take a few risks and go with their committed instincts.

Sales

The record company receives no money for airplay. Sales is everything to a label. The bottom line is units sold.

Writers and publishers are compensated for airplay. The label and the artist, assuming the recording artist did not write the song, are indirect beneficiaries of radio airplay. In general, it is hoped that airplay equals more sales. Ninety-something percent of the buying public buy music because they heard it played on the radio. That being the case, it is extremely important that our products receive airplay.

However, in terms of the previously mentioned bottom line, in terms of what we are really in business to do, we make money only when we sell an album.

Picking the Hits

We don't send our artists out on the road in order for the label to receive feedback as to what songs are liked by various audiences. New artists may not have the opportunity to go on tour until they have already had an album finished and have a single on the radio, which enables them to have a product to go on tour to promote. Sometimes, it's like the horse-before-the-cart adage.

However, an established artist who is out playing on the road may say, "Hey, I got this new song that we just recorded in the studio. It's not out yet but I'd like to play it for you." If the artist, after delivering his new song, receives an overwhelming audience response, certainly the label will take that into consideration when selecting the singles.

We take feedback of any kind into consideration; but we also have years of cumulative experience within the company. These experienced people really have their fingers on the pulse of radio and have tried-and-true, legitimate knowledge as to what songs we should take to the stations.

I have seen instances where it has happened that an artist will have a real strong opinion about what song should be a single and his opinion is contrary to the opinion of people at the label. We are partners with the artist. The artist doesn't work for us, and we don't work for the artist. There is no fiduciary relationship between artist and label. We're equal partners. The artist can take advantage of the experienced people at the label and go along with their recommendations, or if the artist has strong opinions of his own, he may say, "This has got to be the single. I'm positive that this song will get airplay."

I have seen our label defer to the artist's choice, but this occurs strictly on an individual basis—it's not our policy across the board. Whether or not we give the artist such leeway depends on many, many criteria, including the experience of the artist and his level of success.

Sometimes when a record is completed and is turned in to be listened to by the A&R department, we may say, "This is the deal. If we continue with this project, this is how we would like to move forward. We will put this single out, then this single, then this single, because this is what our joint experience tells us will work in this case. If you don't agree, we'll be glad to get out of the way so you can try to find success at another label."

As far as song selection is concerned, the artists have a lot of control over which songs are recorded because they are the ones who have to sell the songs to the public. It is very difficult to make an artist sing a song he doesn't really like. But if the record company, the producer, or someone in A&R feels strongly about a piece of material, they may say to the artist, "Will you just go and try it and let me show you how I think this could work."

We've had experiences where having a positive relationship with the artist has led to the artist trying a song he didn't previously like. Then after recording the song, the artist might say, "See, it just doesn't work for me. I will never like that song." But at other times, after working on a song creatively and artistically with his producer, an artist may say, "Wow. Now I understand why you like this song. It's great. Let's record it." When everyone works together to create positive communication to make a hit product, odds are good that the project will succeed.

In our industry, there is a definite protocol, but there are no rules. Everything is subject to change. After all, we are dealing with art as our commodity; therefore, change is necessary and inevitable.

There are differences in the way we record records with different artists, for instance, a new artist versus Dwight Yoakam. Many times, successful and well-established artists are incredibly in sync with who they are as an artist, the marketplace, their fan base, and so on. A successful relationship with an established artist can be achieved by simply allowing them the creative freedom to continue their success. But not all established artists have total awareness of themselves and their careers. Many times we will continue to guide established artists with their careers in almost the same manner as we guide our newer artists.

Marketing

The problem with statistics, market analysis, and research is that you can make research look like whatever you want. Research can be slanted to various viewpoints, like the Bible, and everyone has a different frame of reference. You can take any fact and manipulate it to reflect your individual slant or interpretation. You may do all of your research and set down your set of parameters only to find out that some of the most successful artists in our business have flown in the face of all the research and analyses thrown at them.

We certainly have a network of consultants, such as radio programmers, who we listen to and whose opinion we value. For example, we may send out a new record to half a dozen people we have solid relationships with to get their feedback. We collect and weigh all information we know to be of value; then we make the final decisions with the artist.

Warner/Chappell

Warner/Chappell is not owned by Warner Bros. Records. Warner/Chappell is a part of Time Warner and part of the Warner Music Group. We are not directly connected to Warner/Chappell, but we are owned by the same parent company.

When searching for the best material for a given album, so many intangibles come into play. For example, if we have a good Warner/Chappell song and a great song from another company, we will record the great song, with all due respect to Warner/Chappell. I would rather have a megahit with a company in which we had no publishing interest than a flop published by a Warner-owned company.

I am very cognizant of our relationship with Warner/Chappell. I would definitely take our relationship into consideration when listening to material, but I've yet to see a decision made that would be contrary to the best long-term interest of the artist. However, it is important to say that I often find great songs from the Warner/Chappell writers because they are talented songwriters who have many hits under their respective belts.

Warner/Chappell is a whole other company from Warner Bros. Records. I have no involvement in selecting songwriters for that company. Tim Wipperman heads up the Warner/Chappell publishing group. Warner/Chappell, like other publishing companies, pitches its writers' material to all of the major labels.

Choosing Songs

There are many variables in selecting songs from outside writers. Burt Bacharach, who does not write for a major publisher but who is acclaimed and esteemed for his great successes, will absolutely be listened to and considered. However, in general, it is our policy not to take songs from unknown writers who send us unsolicited material. The legalities involved in taking in material from unknown sources is quite complex, and we could become vulnerable to infringement lawsuits. For example, if we accept a song from Sony/Tree and we listen to it and our artist listens to it and we decide to pass on it, it is unlikely that we would be faced with illegitimate claims of copyright infringement. I, personally, have never seen the case where a song was stolen just to save six and three-quarters cents on a publishing contract. That is ridiculous. But, unfortunately, all it takes is for us to be accused and to spend a lot of money defending ourselves from a bogus claim.

Additionally, we don't have the physical time to listen to outside material. If we accepted material from all who send it to us, we would be going through approximately 5,000 songs to find one good song, as opposed to going through 500 tapes to find a great song from proven writers. This is an unfortunate situation because I would personally champion the idea of helping a great writer who has never had a song recorded become established; however, helping writers is the job of the publishers.

The wall that gets put up and that keeps outsiders out of our business makes it seem as though getting through or over that wall is impossible. However, if a person has great talent, tenacity, and humility and gets to know some people in our business, it is possible to get past that wall.

The rejection process is necessary. It's part of learning how our business works. Rejections may help a person spend time in Nashville or move to Nashville and become involved in local writers' nights until they have figured out a way to get in the doors. Generally speaking, those people who have enough creativity to get their songs heard are usually very creative people. Getting into our business comes down to the survival of the fittest. I have found that people who are truly motivated will not give up.

Men and Women Artists

If you are going to take the position that there are more men signed than women, then I would take the position that male artists, not individually but collectively, sell more records and sell more concert tickets than the aggregate of female artists. I'm not focusing on any particular female artist because Shania Twain is outselling a lot of male artists, as are Reba McEntire, Faith Hill, and Mindy McCready.

I think we go through cycles of signing males and females. For a while, you couldn't get arrested if you were a female artist because males sold so many more records, but that is changing.

We have many more male artists signed to a roster, both on Warner Bros. and on Reprise, than we have females. A few of our male artists are Paul Brandt, Dwight Yoakam, Michael Peterson, Travis Tritt, David Ball, and Brady Seals. On our roster of female artists, we have Anita Cochran and Faith Hill. That's all we currently have. Right now, I'd rather be a female looking for a deal because we are looking for female artists. If we found a great female artist, we would sign her in a heartbeat because of our lack of female artists.

An Artist's Age

I would say that an artist's age is somewhat of a factor. If great music came through the door and it was unique and deserved to be heard, we would definitely consider it regardless of the age of the artist. In fact, Jim Ed Norman signed a gospel group called the Fairfield Four, and they were all in their seventies or eighties. They won a Grammy award in 1998. The group has been together for fifty years, and the average age is seventy-something.

This is an extreme example. When you start thinking about the age of artists in mainstream country music, you should consider that the age of the average record buyer is fourteen to thirty-five. Naturally, youthful audiences relate to artists who are in their age-group. The consumers want to hear lyrics applicable to their lifestyle and generation sung by someone with whom they may be able to relate.

Also, videos for the majority of the buying public present youthful images of attractive men and women in contemporary situations. Audiences connect with these artists either by living vicariously through their images or by relating to the artist through the message that artist is conveying in his songs.

Definitions

We have a department in our company we refer to as "artist development." Janice Azrak, who heads up our video department, is also in charge of artist development. She spends a considerable amount of time with each artist and gets to know their individual personalities. After Janice is familiar with who the artist is, she then helps them to develop their image as a recording artist.

Philosophically, the artists define themselves. Ultimately, the final image must be a genuine extension of that artist's best traits and characteristics. It is far better to work with a new artist who is appealing and talented rather than trying to change the basic personality of an artist if he doesn't have a positive image. If an artist is misrepresented or represented in a way that is not genuine, it won't be long before the public catches on.

Diversity in Radio

I would like to see country radio stations have a much broader format, similar to the formats in pop music. In pop music, there are several different formats: R&B, alternative, adult contemporary, rock, and so on. All of these formats are played on the radio. We have very different artists, from Randy Travis to the Thompson Brothers and Shania Twain. I would really like to see more specific formats within the country format. I would like to hear George Jones as well as hearing music from Kim Richey.

For a while, I thought radio was moving into a broader scope of airplay with Americana and Triple A radio, which were more accepting of unique artists like Dwight Yoakam, the Thompson Brothers, and Mary Chapin Carpenter. Some stations are more traditional, others play more contemporary country artists, and there are a few stations playing rock or jammin' country music.

I strongly believe that stations with a more liberal format are helping to broaden the base of country music in general. Also, at this time, there are not a lot of places a person can go to hear pure traditional country music because many of the stations are playing records by current contemporary artists.

Perhaps the term "country music" is limiting. I could imagine a name change for country music to American music—then we could divide American music into different formats, such as traditional/country, pop/country, or jammin'/country.

Radio in Europe

European radio stations are quite varied. Rock 'n roll is played back to back with traditional country music. Bob Saporiti was head of our international department for many years. Bob currently heads up our Warner Bros. label. He has a great deal of experience in dealing with foreign country markets.

Future Goals

At the risk of sounding altruistic, my primary goal is not to become a record label president. I enjoy being involved in creating great music that is enjoyed by many people.

Music has moved me. Specific songs have changed my life, music has played a very dramatic role in my life, and I feel a deep need to be a part of making that opportunity available to others. I would like to see others have the chance to enjoy music to the same level and the same degree that I have had the privilege of doing in my life. Therefore, every day I try to succeed in my goal: being a part of the process of creating great music for others to enjoy.

3

Lynn Shults

United Artists, Capitol, and Atlantic Records

Courtesy of Richard Crichton

The worst bankrupt in the world is the man who has lost his enthusiasm. Let him lose everything but enthusiasm and he will come through again to success.

—Anonymous

About United Artists

P rior to a wave of new construction that swept across Nashville's music community in the early 1990s, the most distinctive building was an octagonal, nine-story structure known as the United Artists (UA) Tower. It owed its existence to a record label that hit its peak in the late 1970s behind the steam of Kenny Rogers, but UA had been dormant for more than a decade when that early 1990s construction took place.

United Artists was actually a film company for four decades before it ever became a record label. Actors Charlie Chaplin, Mary Pickford, and Douglas Fairbanks Sr. joined with film mogul D. W. Griffith to form United Artists in 1919 in an effort to bring Hollywood's power into the hands of the creative artists rather than the moneymen.

It did not work out quite as planned. Their early pictures were collectively uneven, and the stars' output was comparatively low in volume. The addition of producer Sam Goldwyn provided a shot in the arm for the film house in the mid-1920s, and UA was able to amass such significant pictures as *Wuthering Heights, Stagecoach,* the original *A Star Is Born,* and the first Alfred Hitchcock picture, *Rebecca.*

By 1950, UA was again in trouble. Reportedly losing $100,000 a week, the company brought entertainment lawyers Arthur Krim and Robert Benjamin on board to change the studio's image. They turned the company around by returning to the independent ideal that underscored UA's formation, allowing producers to bring projects to them. United Artists made quick headway with such films as *The Man with The Golden Arm, Around the World in 80 Days, Some Like It Hot,* and *High Noon.* By 1956, the company had become so successful that Pickford and Chaplin, the two living founders, agreed to sell their interests for $3 million each. United Artists continued to make significant pictures, including the James Bond series, the *Rocky* flicks, and others.

During the Krim/Benjamin years, UA expanded from movies into music, establishing a record label in the early 1960s. Within the first two years, the company scored its first number 1 pop single with the High-waymen's "Michael." When "Michael" slipped out of number 1, it was followed by Bobby Vee's "Take Good Care of My Baby," released by Liberty Records. Liberty's succession of UA would prove ironic several decades later. Other number 1 UA pop recordings included Bobby Goldsboro's "Honey" in 1968, Don McLean's classic "American Pie" in 1972, Paul Anka's "You're Having My Baby" in 1974, and Bill Conti's "Gonna Fly Now" from the first *Rocky* picture, in 1977.

United Artists' West Coast birth did not dissuade the label from working in the field where Nashville dominated. The label's first country chart entry came in 1962, and UA made a major splash with that first release. George Jones, already distinguished with such titles as "Tender Years," "White Lightning," and "Why Baby Why," weaved a believable tale of self-delusion in "She Thinks I Still Care," and the record managed to top the country chart for a lofty six weeks. Jones stayed with the label through 1965, yielding several more hits, including his landmark "The Race Is On." United Artists also earned a fair amount of success with Johnny Darrel, Melba Montgomery, and Del Reeves, who had the label's second number 1 single in 1965, with "Girl on the Billboard."

The San Francisco–based TransAmerica Corporation bought both the film and the record divisions of UA in 1968 and maintained control of the label during the next decade. It was during that time that the UA Tower was built at 50 Music Square West, giving UA an instant recognizability for visitors to Music Row.

The UA Tower coincided with the most productive period in the label's Nashville history. Record producer Larry Butler, who had worked for several years as Johnny Cash's musical director, came on board in 1973, signing such acts as songwriter Dick Feller, Ed Bruce, Billie Jo Spears, and Jean Shepard. Butler's most successful moves were the signings of Kenny Rogers, Crystal Gayle, and Dottie West. Rogers, who had come to prominence as the lead singer for the country/rock group First Edition, was down on his luck, but Butler believed strongly that his uniquely scratchy voice could find a place in country music.

After two other UA artists turned down a song called "Lucille," Butler brought it in at the end of a recording session for Rogers, who didn't believe they had enough time to record the song. They recorded the song in fifteen minutes, and the barroom-story song turned Rogers into a superstar practically overnight. It sold one million copies and led to one of the most successful commercial runs in country music history. Rogers reeled off "The Gambler," "Daytime Friends," "She Believes in Me," "Coward of the County," and "Don't Fall in Love with a Dreamer" (a duet with Kim Carnes), among others, leading Butler to become the first Nashvillian to win the Grammy award for producer of the year in 1980.

Each of the previously mentioned records managed to find a home in pop music as well as country, something UA singer Crystal Gayle was likewise able to do. The youngest sister of Loretta Lynn, Gayle embraced a pop country sound rather than the raw, in-your-face style of her older sibling. Her melodic sensibilities led to hits, beginning in 1974 with "Wrong Road Again" and running through such titles as "I'll Do It All Over Again," "I'll Get Over You," "Talking in Your Sleep," and "Why Have You Left the One You Left Me For." Her biggest success came with "Don't It Make My Brown Eyes Blue." With a classy, torchy piano intro and its clever turn of a phrase, Gayle ascended to number 2 on the pop charts and sold one million copies of the single, eventually leaving UA two years later for a contract with Columbia Records.

Dottie West was the other major success of the Butler era, triggered in part by a handful of duets with Rogers. She found success on her own with the slightly funky "A Lesson in Leavin'" and a sassy public image.

TransAmerica sold UA in April 1978 for $30 million to music executives Artie Mogull and Jerry Rubinstein. The deal came through financing by the British conglomerate EMI, which owned Capitol Records, and Capitol began distributing UA one month after the purchase. In December, Lynn Shults, who succeeded Butler when the producer went independent, left UA to run Capitol. The following February, Mogull and Rubinstein sold UA to EMI.

EMI had gained the catalog of Liberty Records, the label that had followed UA into the top slot on the pop charts back in 1961. Beginning September 22, 1980, UA officially became Liberty Records, and Rogers's *Greatest Hits,* released four days later, was the first album to sport the new label, complete with a Statue of Liberty image. Within three years, Liberty was phased out, with all of the EMI-distributed artists assigned to the Capitol roster. Liberty did, however, make a comeback for several years in the 1990s, when Jimmy Bowen, then head of Capitol, decided to rename the label as Liberty to differentiate it from the pop division of the label. However, when Scott Hendricks replaced Bowen in 1995, his first move was to reinstate Capitol as the company's name.

In the latter part of 1998, the UA name was still affixed to the Tower on Music Row, though the label sold it off years ago. The best-known companies to occupy the building today are the fan magazine *The Music City News* and Loud Recording Studio, owned by DreamWorks executive James Stroud, who has used the studio to record Tim McGraw, Tracy Lawrence, and Clay Walker.

Lynn Shults at United Artists

In 1973, I went to work for United Artists. United Artists was a big corporation headquartered in Los Angeles and New York. There was United Artists Films, United Artists Publishing, and the country wing in Nashville. They were located on Music Row, on 17th Avenue, and Del Reeves was their big act. There were only four people in the office when I came on board, and Kelso Herston was the head of the label. Kelso hired me to be head of national promotions and sales manager for our country product. I was paid about $25,000 a year; there were bonuses, but there was no structured percentage. Before then, I had worked for Acuff-Rose and others since the mid-1960s.

The first artist I was ever able to be a part of signing at United Artists was Crystal Gayle in 1973. I'd gone out to the old WSM television studios with one of our artists, and Crystal was rehearsing for a television show that was being produced there. Along with some other people, I was waiting in a small room that had a television monitor in it, when all of a sudden I look up at the monitor and I see this incredibly beautiful, very young woman. I think to myself, "Wow, who is that?" I left the little room and went into the studio so I could hear her sing, and I thought, "God, she is great!"

Later, I asked someone who worked there, "Who is that?" He said, "That's Crystal Gayle, Loretta's little sister." I said, "You mean Loretta Lynn's little sister? Is she signed to anybody?" He said, "Yeah, she has a deal over at Decca Records." [At that time, MCA (Music Corporation of America) was called Decca Records. Today, the Nashville label division is called Decca/MCA.]

I introduced myself to Crystal that afternoon. I did not let go of the visual image of her or her voice; she was great. She was not a clone of anyone else. I followed up with phone calls. Decca Records had released three singles on Crystal that had charted on the *Billboard* charts, but they didn't have any significant success. The label's executives were interested in Loretta, not her little sister.

So I went on a campaign with Kelso Herston to get Crystal signed. I introduced Crystal to Kelso, he listened to her sing, and he agreed to sign her. I didn't have the actual power to sign her—I just badgered Kelso into signing her.

After I had convinced Kelso to sign Crystal, Kelso left United Artists. Then Larry Butler, who was a well-known and greatly respected producer, came in and headed up the label. Larry and I sat and talked, and I didn't think that Larry was the right producer for Crystal, nor did Larry. So Larry said, "Who do you think should produce Crystal?" I said, "Allen Reynolds."

I'd known Allen for a while, and we were friends, but more importantly, I'd seen Allen produce artists and greatly admired him. Allen Reynolds is a hell of a guy. In many ways, the word "producer" says that you're the boss, and therefore you do things the producer's way. And there have been a lot of people who have produced a lot of records in this town that way and some that still do. But Allen goes about producing by finding out what the artist is all about and where the artist is the most comfortable, then creating as great an environment as he can to help that artist be all he can be. That is why I suggested to Garth Brooks and Crystal Gayle that they speak with Allen about producing their records.

Allen and Crystal had a string of great hit records. The greatest classic song that came out of this liaison was "Don't It Make My Brown Eyes Blue," written by Richard Leigh.

The story about that song goes like this. A songwriter, Sandy Mason, had gotten to know Allen and Richard as friends. She suggested to Richard that he play some of his material for Allen. So Richard goes over to Allen's and plays his songs for him. After listening to several of Richard's songs, Allen said, "I don't really hear anything I can use right now." So they're standing at the door saying their good-byes and all of a sudden, out of the blue, Allen asks Richard, "Well, have you got any other songs?" Richard says, "Well, I've got one more, but I don't really think it's what you're looking for."

At that point, most people would have said, "Well, okay, I really enjoyed it, and see you later," and out the door the writer would have gone. But Allen says to Richard, "Well, let me hear it." So Richard played his last song for Allen, and that song just happened to be "Don't It Make My Brown Eyes Blue." That song made Crystal a huge star, won a Grammy for Richard, crossed over to the pop charts, and is still one of ASCAP's most performed songs.

At the same time that all this is happening at United Artists, a guy calls for an appointment, walks into Larry's office, and says, "I want to make some country records." Larry says, "Well, okay." So Larry called Mike

Stewart, his boss in Los Angeles, and says, "Kenny Rogers just walked in, and he wants to makes some country records." Mike said, "Are you crazy?" Larry says, "No, I really would like to record him." So they discussed this back and forth for a while, then Mike gave Larry the go-ahead to sign Kenny to United Artists.

Ken Kragen was Kenny's manager. Ken was a dedicated manager and truly an asset to Kenny's career.

On December 13, 1975, Kenny charted with his first single, "Love Lifted Me," which made it only to number 19 on the *Billboard* charts, but it was the beginning of Kenny's country career. Eighteen months later, on January 29, 1977, Kenny charted with another song called "Lucille," written by Roger Bowling and Paul Richey. So the label got hot quickly. Crystal was on her third album. Her first number 1 single was "I'll Get Over You" in the summer of 1976, and "Don't It Make My Brown Eyes Blue" hit the charts on July 9, 1977. But these artists were growing fast and exploded into superstars. They exploded like rockets. This was an incredible time. Also, in the midst of all this, Dottie West, who was also signed to United Artists, and Kenny had huge duet hits. Their first duet, "Every Time Two Fools Collide," charted on February 18, 1978, and went to number 1 on the *Billboard* charts, just one year behind "Lucille."

Singles, in part, are determined by audience response when artists are on the road performing songs from their new albums. Back in the days we're talking about, the type of market research used now didn't exist. It's been my experience that research often misses the big hit songs, and I still believe that the intuition of a few key people is the best selector for the singles.

Singles are selected by the opinions of the artist, the artist's manager, the record producer, and the label head, if the label head has a background in picking hit songs. If he doesn't, he may defer his vote to the head of his A&R department or the head of his promotion department. Normally, between three and five people at the core of the artist's project select the singles by their experience and intuition. They better not be playing publishing games, better not be getting greedy, and better use their pulse and their intuition as the guiding radar to lead them to the right songs.

We had enormously talented artists going on concert tours together: Kenny Rogers, Dottie West, and Crystal Gayle. Working with them was an incredible experience. They would be booked into the big arenas, and they'd be sold out with people hanging from the rafters.

Crystal's first manager was not a nice guy. He was a real jerk. He was not a part of the country culture and he acted as though we were all a bunch of illiterate hillbillies. When Crystal did the *Tonight Show* with Johnny Carson, he acted like he was the cock of the walk. He was obnoxious. No one wanted to be around him. Consequently, he didn't last very long, and he is not around the business today.

Bill Gatzimos, Crystal's husband and second manager, was a law student at Vanderbilt University when we first signed Crystal, so Bill couldn't go out on the road with her as much as he wanted to. So I went out with Crystal when Bill couldn't go. Through the years, Bill, Crystal, and I spent a lot of time together and became good friends.

She didn't have her own band; we'd go into the venues, and she had to sing in front of the house bands, most of which were pretty bad. She had to change her costumes under horrible conditions—in the club's bathroom or a small office. These were not the best of conditions. I got to see Crystal grow from those days to the point in time where she put her own band together and traveled comfortably.

I'll always remember Crystal telling me that she didn't want her life to be like Loretta's, meaning that she didn't want to be on the road 250 days a year. I told her, "Crystal, it doesn't have to be that way." Bill, Crystal, and I had a meeting. I was saying, "Crystal, you need to figure out at what level you can live comfortably and how much money you'll need to live as you want to. Then figure out how many dates, on the road, you're going to have to meet in order to make that much money. If it's more dates than you want, you're going to have to reduce your standard of living a little bit."

In those days, Crystal was being paid about $2,500 per performance date. However, it wasn't long before she was making $5,000 per date and then $10,000; then all of a sudden she was getting $25,000 to $50,000 per performance. Things were happening pretty fast for Crystal.

Bill and Crystal decided that they wanted a marriage of quality, and they wanted a family, so early on in her career Crystal drew a line as to how many times she would go out on the road. The first year she worked a lot of dates. After that she decided that about eighty dates a year was comfortable for her, so that's how many dates she worked.

I was in my thirties when I was working with the hottest country acts in the country. Those days were unbelievable. I'm honored to have worked with Kenny Rogers, Dottie West, Crystal Gayle, and many others. They were all very nice people. There was never a time when anyone ever raised their voice. They were kind and generous to all the people who worked for them, regardless of that person's status, power, or job criteria.

Under the Umbrella, It Sometimes Rained

Under the umbrella of the record label, it sometimes rained a lot. There were disagreements between various in-house departments. There's an unspoken rule that people in publishing and people in A&R do not get along. [The publishers want to recoup the draw the writers are getting, the writers want their songs cut, and the A&R people want the artist to cut the best songs they can find, wherever that might be.] There's a lot of conflict and power struggles, which make for some strongly adversarial relationships within the label departments. There is always that feeling in a conflict situation, "That we're in the same company, so your artist should be recording our staff writer's songs." [The corporations that own the labels set up the publishing company divisions in order to make as much money as they possibly can by not only taking a percentage from their artists but also receiving royalty payments from their staff writers whenever their artists cut the staff writers' songs.]

There will be periods when you will hear superb products on the radio, then there will be cycles when everything is off; 80 percent of success comes out of 20 percent effort.

An artist should cut only the best songs for them. But there is a thing called greed that is a part of human nature, and I don't know how to prevent it from creeping into the cracks through anyone's walls.

Transitions

In 1976, as I previously mentioned, I left United Artists and worked at RCA for a while. Jerry Bradley, who was the head of RCA/Nashville at that time, wanted me to move to New York and work in a liaison position with Nashville. I said to Jerry, "That's just not possible. That would be like trying to grow a row of corn in the middle of Times Square." So I worked at RCA/Nashville for one year, then I went back to United Artists.

In 1969, Capitol/Nashville bought United Artists/Nashville. The famous corporate statement was made: "We're buying this company, but don't worry, there aren't going to be any changes." Then as the buy is in transition, prior to the final purchase, they move me to Capitol. This was unreal. As I look back and think about it, I wonder, "How am I still alive today?"

Frank Jones was a wonderful man who was running Capitol, but Capitol had let Frank go and they had an artist roster of forty-six. So here I am with all these artists and no help. I had been used to United Artist, the little boutique label with a few artists and many hits. During this one-year transitional period, I'm told there's a hands-off policy at United Artists. So I was at Capitol for one year, hands off of United Artists; then, after the buy-out was finalized, everything was once again turned over to me.

About Capitol Records

Capitol Records has an incredible history in the record business. It was the home of the Beatles and the Beach Boys, it became the first company to use all three turntable playing speeds (78, 45, and 33-$\frac{1}{3}$ rpm), and it was the first to send free promotional copies of its product to the nation's disc jockeys in an effort to get free advertising through airplay. However, Capitol is also unusual among record companies that remain successful in Nashville today, because its country division was centered primarily in Los Angeles for much of its history.

Capitol was started on April 8, 1942, by three already established entertainment figures: Johnny Mercer, a songwriter known for such titles as "Autumn Leaves," "You Must Have Been a Beautiful Baby," and "Hooray for Hollywood"; Glenn Wallichs, who owned Wallich's Music City in Hollywood; and Paramount Pictures executive George "Buddy" DeSylva. Like Mercer, DeSylva was also a successful songwriter, with such credits as "Button Up Your Overcoat" and "California, Here I Come."

The three major labels of the time—Columbia, RCA, and Decca—all maintained New York headquarters, but Capitol found success almost immediately, scoring a pair of Top 10 hits by the fall. It became the first successful major label on the West Coast.

Capitol's success was not easily won. A strike by the American Federation of Musicians just two months after the label's creation prevented record companies from recording, led by a fear that sessions were taking away work from stage musicians. Also, a shortage of shellac during World War II had negative consequences. However, Capitol persevered and built its reputation and its financial coffers by accumulating strong talent: Nat King Cole, Peggy Lee, Les Paul and Mary Ford, and Tennessee Ernie Ford, among others. In 1954, the label brought Frank Sinatra on board, giving Capitol an enviable identity with traditional pop.

From the very beginning, Capitol made a conscious effort to include country music in its stylistic stable, signing western hero Tex Ritter in its first year of operation. Ritter had had little success on record in previous efforts, but he teamed with Capitol and racked up a series of national hits, including "Jealous Heart," "Rye Whiskey," "I'm Wastin' My Tears On You," and "You Will Have to Pay." Chicago native Lee Gillette and Cliffie Stone, a 1989 inductee into the Country Music Hall of Fame, served as the label's first talent scouts, building Capitol's country stable around Tennessee Ernie Ford, Merle Travis, Tex Williams, Hank Thompson, and Jimmy Wakely.

In 1951, Ken Nelson succeeded Gillette as the country A&R man, adding such talents as Sonny James, Faron Young, Jean Shepard, Wanda Jackson, Ferlin Husky, Rose Maddox, and the Louvin Brothers.

In the mid-1950s, just as the rock era was getting under way, Capitol built its famous circular office building in Hollywood. One of the most recognizable locations in Los Angeles, it has often been likened to a stack of records, though the building's architect insisted that the design actually reflected an interest in efficiency. For instance, it would cost less to heat a circular office building than a traditional building in which the heat had to find its way into the corners of the rooms.

Capitol had already broken ground on that building when controlling interest was purchased by EMI, a British company, for $8.5 million. EMI's affiliation began January 1, 1995, and is still in place today.

Capitol had some trouble becoming a major player during the rock era, even though Gene Vincent's 1956 rockabilly recording "Be-Bop-a-Lula," a hit in both pop and country music, gave the label an early classic. It wasn't until the advent of the Beatles and the Beach Boys that Capitol was recognized as a major player in the field. Since that time, Capitol has had significant success with the likes of Bob Seger, Natalie Cole, Heart, Tina Turner, Grand Funk, Helen Reddy, and Pink Floyd.

Ken Nelson turned Capitol into one of the powerhouses of the 1960s. Like many of the producers of that day, Nelson took a hands-off approach with his artists, allowing them to pick their own music and develop their own arrangements. He worked more as a consultant and less as a dictator, allowing the artists to hone their own sound.

Sonny James fashioned a remarkable string of sixteen straight number 1 records with Nelson behind the glass. Nelson did particularly well by mining the streets of Bakersfield for Buck Owens, Merle Haggard, and Wynn Steward. Owens successfully combined a rock attitude with country club leanings, making high-energy records at a time when country leaned heavily toward ballads and dark tales.

Haggard emerged as one of the most significant singer-songwriters in the genre's history after his release from prison in 1963. Songs such as "Branded Man," "Okie from Muskogee," "The Fightin' Side of Me," and "Mama Tried" earned him a reputation as the "poet of the common man," as Haggard embodied the concerns and conditions of America's blue-collar class in a bold, sympathetic manner.

Capitol also achieved significant success with a session guitar player who had worked on recordings by Haggard, Sinatra, and the Monkees: Glen Campbell. In the space of about eighteen months, he developed a successful recording career and acquired his own television show, then reeled off a string of lush pop/country recordings: "Wichita Lineman," "Galveston," "By the Time I Get to Phoenix," and "Gentle on My Mind." He would also score big in the 1970s with "Rhinestone Cowboy" and "Southern Nights."

Capitol was the first major record company to establish a Nashville office. However, it held that office under somewhat strict control. Nelson continued to spend most of his time in Los Angeles, and when former Columbia executive Frank Jones was asked to run the label in 1973, he was asked to move to the West Coast. Joe Allison, who wrote the Jim Reeves hit "He'll Have to Go," held down the Nashville office during 1973 and 1974 before Jones's return.

Jones remained in charge of Capitol for five years, then was succeeded by Lynn Shults, who headed the office until 1984. Capitol developed such acts as Anne Murray, Gene Watson, Mel McDaniel, Dan Seals, and Juice Newton, but the bulk of power remained in Los Angeles.

It remained so, in fact, until April 1984, when industry veteran Jim Foglesong was asked to take over the Nashville office. At the time, the label staff had shrunk from fifteen employees to only five, but Foglesong built both the personnel and the roster quickly. Under his reign, Capitol returned to a place of prominence. Foglesong brought on board Tanya Tucker, Barbara Mandrell, T. Graham Brown, Don Williams, Suzy Bogguss, and Sawyer Brown.

In December 1989, Foglesong was replaced by Jimmy Bowen, who, ironically, had also replaced Foglesong at MCA in 1984. Bowen, a controversial figure who had produced standard pop acts such as Sinatra and Dean Martin before moving to Nashville in 1978, oversaw Garth Brooks's most successful period, when "The Dance," "Friends in Low Places," and "Shameless" cemented Bowen's recording prowess, even as Brooks was establishing his own preferences at the label. Even though Bowen had greatly enlarged the marketing budget for Brooks, the two were not a happy couple. Brooks fought with Bowen over the size of his contract, and when Brooks was unable to get the deal he wanted, he went over Bowen's head to Charles Koppelman, who ran the Capitol-EMI operations in North America.

Bowen wanted more autonomy for the Nashville division, so Bowen changed the name of Capitol/Nashville to Liberty Records in 1992, distancing the label from the pop side of music. Bowen also wanted to make Liberty a full-service imprint, signing pop and rock acts as well as country acts. Bowen endured an uneasy tenure until late 1994, when he was diagnosed with cancer. He retired early the next year and moved to Hawaii.

Scott Hendricks, who earned a name by developing hits for Restless Heart, Brooks & Dunn, and John Michael Montgomery, was brought on board to replace Bowen. Hendricks returned the company's name to Capitol, believing that the legacy of the name was more important than distancing the division from Capitol's pop operation.

During his two and a half years, Hendricks broke Trace Adkins and Deana Carter but, he like Bowen, could not get along with Garth Brooks. Brooks was unhappy with his record sales, especially the sales of his album *Fresh Horses*. Brooks blamed the label, which he decided had pulled off its marketing campaign too early. Capitol's New York office was set to handle the marketing of his next album, and a free concert in Central Park in August 1997 was set to provide the *Sevens* album with a huge kick off.

Instead, EMI closed down its New York office, and Brooks found himself with a potential marketing nightmare. Brooks refused to deliver the album, and the conflicts were unresolved until Hendricks agreed to step down from the label in November. Hendricks was replaced by Pat Quigley, a former beer marketer who had played a major role in the development of the Central Park show. Quigley, a promoter more than a businessman, was dispatched to the Nashville office in mid-1997.

In 1998, the first full year of Quigley's reign, Brooks's *Sevens* album was joined by a limited-edition boxed set featuring his previous six-set studio albums, a two-CD live album, and the *Hope Floats* soundtrack, which hinged greatly on Brooks's performance of a Bob Dylan song, "To Make You Feel My Love."

A new Capitol office building that Hendricks had overseen was sold at a loss before Capitol ever moved.

Lynn Shults at Capitol Records

I was vice president of A&R for ten years when I was at Capitol. Major labels are highly competitive because they're always trying to beat their competition. However, in the music business, unlike other big business, because of the many social functions and because there is always a lot of shifting and moving around in the same small circles, people know and come to respect one another.

New York and Los Angeles

I've always had a problem with directives coming from the New York or Los Angeles offices. Companies are set up as profit-making corporations. The final decisions come out of the home offices. Many times those decisions are not in the best interest of their satellite companies. I think that an enormous amount of money has been made in Nashville, and the percentage reinvested back into the community is contributory but not equal. There's been an overload of profits taken out of Nashville and reinvested in other corporate areas.

Another policy I have a problem with is that the home offices only look to Nashville for country music, and Nashville offers all genres of music, not just country. The parent corporations have not looked at Nashville to expand beyond its country scope. I think that is wrong.

On the other side of that premise, some of the powers in Nashville don't want Nashville to expand into other music markets because they think that other music markets may become an economic threat to their country companies. It's all about economic power. There are people in Nashville who don't want to rock the boat; they prefer the status quo.

It's ironic that last year three of the Top 10 records on the *Billboard* pop charts all came out of Nashville. There's a tremendous amount of creative talent in Nashville that is not being properly exploited by the home offices.

I think it's just a damn shame that the powers-that-be continue to keep Nashville's product strictly country.

Dominant Departments

All the major labels are basically set up with the same internal structures. When the head of a label is a producer, the label will be dominated by the A&R department, and the people in the other departments will, at times, feel as though they are getting the short end of the stick. When the guy running the label comes from a promotion/marketing background, people in other departments believe that promotion and marketing are receiving too much attention and money and are consequently frustrating the creative ability of the A&R department.

The problem is not in how the labels are structured, but with the people who head the labels and the departments. There are some people who have great intuition in picking hit songs; they tend to be able to understand what the public wants, and deliver the appropriate response to radio. They know when, where, and why to pump more money into certain projects and when not to. The problem comes when the department heads don't have this intuition and pump money and time into failing projects. I think you've got to have people who really have strong intuitive powers in many different areas.

If I could restructure the labels, I wouldn't have producers as label heads (as a rule; there are always exceptions). This is because producers have never been in the trenches getting records played on the radio. They don't have the sales and marketing background, both inside and outside of the company. The music business is like a giant maze, and success requires a lot of strong relationships in many varied areas. Achieving desired end results requires a tremendous amount of financing in both promotion and marketing to make a project successful. Producers don't have an in-depth knowledge in these areas.

In the current system, success has been achieved under diverse circumstances, but I think greater success could be achieved if more than one person were involved in critical decision making. There should be three to five people working as a team in the decision-making process. But I do believe that, after all the input has been thoroughly discussed and absorbed, the label head must make the final call.

Some may think that there is too much power in the hands of one person, but if that person is a really good leader and does not abuse the power he has and delegates some of that power to the people in those fields of expertise, then the system works very well. Departments should be facilitators for one another all working together cooperatively to achieve success for each project. This can be achieved if the label head empowers his people in various departments.

Radio

Radio, contrary to what a lot of people might think, is always looking for new artists and new music. Radio is looking for the music and the artist generating the most excitement. The more excitement is generated, the more people will listen. The more listeners a station has is directly related to the amount of advertising revenue generated for the station.

Sales

To a record company, sales are everything. If you don't sell, you don't get paid. No money exchanges hands unless a unit is sold. Technically, the only people who are making money from radio airplay are the publishers and the songwriters. However, airplay creates the opportunity for units to be sold.

Radio works with the labels. A record company presents a radio station with a new artist, and sometimes radio likes that artist, and sometimes they don't. If you have had a good and long-term relationship with that station and have developed the trust factor, then in certain situations that station will help you by playing your artists' records. If that station is in a large market and is involved in a big ratings battle, or if the person you are dealing with doesn't have the latitude to give you a break, then your record won't be played. [Record promoters who are in-house are paid a salary; promoters who do not work for the record labels are paid as independent contractors. The job of the promoter is to call on large-market radio stations to receive airplay for the records they are promoting.]

Since the major labels are well financed, their products have a greater chance of receiving airplay than the smaller, independent labels, which don't have the financing to pay for large-scale record promotion. Promoters call on radio stations and try to get their records played. Labels hire in-house record promoters. There is usually one person who is the head of national promotion who works with four or five other promotion people. When these people are combined with other label people, all working for the label's product, there can be as many as ten to fifteen people directly and indirectly involved in the promotion department.

Radio program directors decide what product to play by their personal expertise and by using outside consultants. Radio stations hire research consultants who survey listeners and concertgoers to determine which performers and songs are best liked.

The people who are called on by the researchers select product the same way a person might select a loaf of bread in a grocery store. People select different products because of price, brand name, visual appeal, and so on.

Males and Females

In the past, record labels signed more men than women for various reasons. The most obvious reason was because there were more men than women vying to be stars. Also, the parents of most young girls will not allow them to sing in bars and nightclubs, which is understandable. The men, however, have gone out with their fathers or their families at a very early age and began to sing in bars and nightclubs.

Now, all of this reasoning can be thrown out the window. It no longer is true, as more and more women, with a broad format range from country to pop, are appealing to female record buyers. For instance, LeAnn Rimes, Shania Twain, Trisha Yearwood, and many more women are signed to major labels and playing dominant roles in the industry.

Vice President of A&R

I went over to Capitol in 1978 shortly before the sale of United Artists in 1979. For a ten-year period at Capitol, I was responsible for signing artists, determining what songs would be recorded, heading up the sales and promotions departments, and combining the rosters.

The criteria I used for signing artists, aside from my years of experience, was subjective. I signed artists if I believed their talent was great enough and unique enough to be profitable for the label. The age of an artist didn't enter into my selection process. In fact, on one occasion, I got into trouble for wanting to sign an artist who was young. She was fourteen years old. I think it's ironic that Mike Curb has had three huge successes with three thirteen-year-old girls: Debby Boone, Marie Osmond, and LeAnn Rimes. I tried to sign a fourteen-year-old to Capitol and was almost crucified by my legal department. They didn't want to deal with a minor because of all the liability connected with signing a minor.

During my years at Capitol, many great artists were signed. One was Tanya Tucker, who had previously been signed to MCA and Arista Records. She was twenty-eight years old when she signed with Capitol and was considered, by some, to be washed up. Tanya's first single release on Capitol debuted on February 15, 1986, and from that point on, Tanya became a legend in the music arena.

Another artist was Dan Seals. His first single, "Everybody's Dream Girl," charted on April 30, 1983. "Meet Me in Montana," a duet with Marie Osmond, was Dan's first song to go to number 1 on the *Billboard* country charts. Sawyer Brown was signed to a production deal by Curb Records, but I made a deal with Mike Curb to sign Sawyer Brown to Capitol Records. Once Sawyer Brown had been signed to our label, I assigned Randy Scruggs to produce the band, and Mike Curb, Dick Whitehouse, Jim Foglesong, and Sawyer Brown all agreed with the decision. Mike Curb still owned Sawyer Brown via his production contract, but Sawyer Brown was now signed to Capitol as a Capitol recording artist.

Mike Curb made similar agreements with other major labels. Even though Mike had RCA/Curb, MCA/Curb, Capitol/Curb, and so on, those terms were just a matter of semantics. The Judds were on RCA's label like Sawyer Brown was on Capitol's label. In other words, if you went into a record store and picked up the physical record, you would see that the Judds were on RCA, Sawyer Brown was on Capitol, Marie Osmond was on Capitol, and the small print indicated "Mike Curb" or "Curb Productions."

Dan Seals was terrific. When Dan was a pop star, he was part of the duo known as England Dan and John Ford Coley. My relationships with Dan, Tony Gottlieb, his manager, and Kyle Lehning, who produced Dan, were very special to me.

I've been asked, "What makes these artists different from other artists?" The answer is, they were fun to be around, yet they were totally professional as artists. They were extremely talented. They had no egotistical attitudes whatsoever.

For instance, when Anne Murray would walk into a business meeting, her attitude was, "Okay, I'm here. Now what are we going to do about Anny Murray today?" She would speak of herself as a third person, Anne Murray, the artist. She was able to divorce Anne Murray, the person, the wife, the mother of two children, the friend, the daughter who dearly loved her mother and father, the sister who loved her brothers and sisters, from Anne Murray, the artist, a product to be marketed and to be dealt with in a businesslike manner.

Many artists have trauma and terrible stage fright prior to going on stage. One of the aspects that always amazed me about Anne was that the entire time she was backstage waiting to go on, she was as comfortable as if she were sitting in a lawn chair in her backyard and remained totally Anne, the person, until she actually walked into the wings. Then you'd see this incredible transformation take place as Anne Murray, the person, turned into Anne Murray, the consummate performer. Yet Anne remained warm, giving, considerate, and wonderful to be around. If there ever was anyone who could have justified a big ego regarding status, power, and talent, Anne had every right to, but she never became self-indulgent.

Marie Osmond, Tanya Tucker, and Juice Newton were also a lot of fun to work with. Marie hit big in 1973, at the age of thirteen, with "Paper Roses." The song went number 1 on the *Billboard* country charts. She began performing with her brothers when she was fourteen. Capitol's association with the Osmonds was also with Mike Curb. Marie came over to Capitol Records through a production agreement with Mike Curb.

Marie had been on Polydor, MGM Records, Elektra, and RCA, but she wasn't getting any hits. She'd had the huge "Paper Roses" hit, and then nothing was happening for her. My theory regarding Marie's not getting hit songs involves my ego. I believe I have the wonderful gift of intuition, which cannot be documented, in matching the right artist with the right song with the right producer, then taking those components and nurturing and combining them, which enables the artist to be the very best they can be. When Jim Fogelsong [the president of Capitol at that time] and myself met with Marie and her manager, Karl Ingemann, I thought, "You know, I bet we can pull this off. I bet we can really get Marie a hit."

In 1984, I teamed Marie with Paul Worley [vice president of Columbia] to produce her and Ed Saey [an independent producer and studio engineer] to be her studio engineer. The first single we released on Marie was a song called "Until I Fall in Love Again," and we shot ourselves in the foot because the song peaked at number 54 in *Billboard.* Needless to say, we were pretty upset. There were a lot of people who were laughing at our non-success, because the word was out that "this guy [meaning me] thought he could really pull this off."

We regrouped, and in time I found a wonderful song by Paul Davis, who was a fine artist in his own right, along with being a superlative songwriter. I had ten consecutive number 1 songs with my artists performing songs written by Paul. The song Paul had was called "Meet Me in Montana." Then I decided that this song should be performed as a duet with Dan Seals. Dan wasn't quite sure he wanted to do a duet with Marie because Dan was enjoying a great deal of success at that time and Marie was just not making it. Kyle was also unsure about the project. There was no doubt on Marie's part. She wanted to do the song with Dan. Finally, we got Dan and Marie in the studio with that wonderful song. It was absolute magic, and the rest is history. In 1985, Marie Osmond returned to number 1 on the *Billboard* country chart with this duet.

I put all of that together. I was the team leader. We followed that up with another number 1, "There's No Stopping Your Heart," a number 4 called "Read My Lips," and another number 1 with a duet with Marie and Paul Davis called "You're Still New to Me" in 1986, a song written by Paul. Then, for whatever the reason, the magic got lost; but we did pull it off, and it was a great run. The entire Osmond clan are terrific people as well as extremely talented artists.

Leaving Capitol

Capitol was the scene of the most significant trauma I have ever had to deal with in my professional career. In December 1989, our entire staff was replaced when Jimmy Bowen took over operations at the label. He cleaned house. I was let go, along with many other employees.

Bowen and I have known each other for a long time, and I have a great deal of respect for him in many ways. At that particular time, Jimmy Bowen was fighting for his professional survival; he had been tossed out of MCA, so he had to find something to do. He was tremendously aggressive, and he had support from inside corporate sources, particularly Joe Smith, who was Capitol's CEO, and there was no allegiance to any of us in Nashville. I don't think there was anything anyone could have done that would have prevented this unbelievable upheaval. It was in the cards, and that's the way it was.

To this day, I still believe that was one of the greatest wrongs that has ever been done, and not just on my behalf. We had a great staff and artist roster. We had had a lot of success. Nashville was in a transitional state from 1987 through 1989, and country music was floundering. But I had just signed Garth Brooks to Capitol and I knew we were getting ready to explode. What I lived for was pulled right out from under me. I try to live by the quote, "Good people make good things happen," and we had a tremendous amount of good people on our staff and on our artist roster; these people did not deserve what happened to them. Combined with that, my marriage was falling apart, and I had horrible health problems in 1988. I'd never had to deal with any major league adversities like the ones that hammered me at Capitol.

I decided to go into counseling to find out what made me tick, and people who have gone through that understand the process. It's a fascinating journey because you find out a lot about yourself, but there's a lot of stuff I didn't really want to find out about as I began connecting the dots of my personality. It's frightening. Now my attitude is, that everything that happened was meant to be, and that's just it. It was meant to be, and it happened.

About Atlantic Records

Country music has often been referred to as the "white man's blues," yet it still took more than forty years for Atlantic Records, which first gained notoriety as an R&B label, to make a successful entry into country. Not that Atlantic didn't try before. The label had a couple of false starts before it opened in Nashville in 1989.

Atlantic's history dates back to October 1947, when it was founded as a jazz label. Almet Ertegun, who'd moved to the United States in 1934 when his father, Munir Ertegun, was named Turkey's ambassador to the United States, used $10,000 invested by his dentist, Dr. Vahdi Sabit, to form Atlantic with Herb Abramson of National Records.

Atlantic would become a historic label in jazz history, issuing the music of John Coltrane, Ornette Coleman, and Charles Mingus, among others, as it established its first significant niche in R&B. In 1949, Stick McGhee gave the record company its first national hit record, "Drinking Wine, Spo-Dee-O-Dee, Drinking Wine" (the first song that future rock/country star Jerry Lee Lewis ever sang in public). This prompted Ertegun and Abramson to tour the South looking for more rhythm and blues talent to sign.

In the ensuing years, Atlantic brought such acts as Ruth Brown, the Clovers, Ben E. King, the Drifters, and one Ray Charles into the national consciousness. Charles, in fact, would become a major force in revitalizing country at a time when the music was struggling. Following the advent of rock 'n roll in the late 1950s, country hit a slump, and one of Music City's reactions was the creation of the "Nashville sound" by Chet Atkins, Owen and Harold Bradley, and a small handful of others, softening the twangy edges in favor of more mass-appeal pop sounds. At the same time, Charles decided to make an album of country standards. Charles was by then recording for ABC-Paramount when he recorded *Modern Sounds in Country and Western Music* in 1962. Many of those around him believed it was a huge mistake, that in a racially divided

American culture, his black core audience would desert him in waves. Instead, renditions of "You Don't Know Me" and "I Can't Stop Loving You" further built his white following and afforded added respect for country music across the entire culture.

While Charles was expanding the reach of country music, Atlantic extended the reach of the label in the late 1950s and 1960s through the signing of Bobby Darin. Darin expected little when the company convinced him to record a novelty tune, but "Splish Splash" became a major rock 'n roll hit for him. Follow-up hits "Dream Lover" and "Mack The Knife" put him in a more traditional pop vocal vein.

Darin's success led to a succession of pop and rock coups. One of Darin's session players introduced Ertegun to Sonny and Cher, and their managers in turn led Atlantic to Buffalo and Springfield, leading to Crosby, Stills, Nash and Young. The ongoing R&B success of Atlantic, which now included Aretha Franklin, Wilson Pickett, and Otis Redding (the latter through a deal with the Memphis-based Stax Records), made the label a powerhouse in pop culture.

In late 1967, Atlantic was sold to Warner Bros./Seven Arts for $17.5 million, a figure that many felt was well below market value. Indeed, in 1968, Ertegun offered $40 million to buy the company back and was rebuffed. Instead, Warner/Seven Arts was sold to Kinney National Service for $400 million, placing Steven Ross, who had attained wealth in the funeral business, in charge of Atlantic's future.

Ertegun had every intention of leaving the company, but Ross surprised Ertegun with his musical knowledge and convinced him to stay, promising him autonomy to run Atlantic as he saw fit. Through the 1970s, Ertegun saw the company through a period that brought the world Led Zeppelin, the Bee Gees, Roberta Flack, Genesis, the Spinners, Chic, Foreigner, and many more.

The 1970s also brought Atlantic's first forays into country music, led by Jerry Wexler, who had joined Atlantic's ownership in 1953. Wexler produced many of the company's acts, Wilson Pickett and Aretha Franklin among them, and he was charged with establishing a Nashville outpost for Atlantic during the early part of the 1970s. Rick Sanjek was appointed head of the office when it opened in 1972, and the roster included John Prine, Doug Sahm, Henson Cargill, and Willie Nelson.

Nelson, working out of Texas, managed to reach the country chart on five different occasions with Wexler producing. Two of those singles, "Bloody Mary Morning" and "After the Fire Is Gone," a duet with unrelated Tracy Nelson, reached the Top 20. More important, however, his two Atlantic albums, *Shotgun Willie* and *Phases and Stages,* have emerged as milestones in Nelson's career, setting up the recording approach that would bring him to superstardom after joining Columbia Records in 1975.

Then Atlantic abandoned Nashville, waiting until the 1980s to give country music another try, this time operating out of its West Coast offices with the subsidiary Atlantic America label. With the California approach to country, the label squeezed out five Top 20 singles for Glen Campbell between 1982 and 1986, including "Faithless Love," a remake of the Brook Benton standard "It's Just a Matter of Time," and the Top 5 ballad "A Lady Like You." Billy Joe Royal took up where Campbell left off, adding eight more Top 20 singles for Atlantic America from 1985 to 1989, including "Love Has No Right," "Burned Like a Rocket," and a remake of Aaron Neville's "Tell It Like It Is."

Knowing that the company was capable of making inroads in country at that point in time, Atlantic chose to once again open a Nashville office in 1989. Rick Blackburn was chosen to run the label, a particularly interesting choice because he had for seven years headed the CBS Records office in Nashville. During that time, he signed Ray Charles, the former Atlantic artist, in a move that was considered controversial. Music Row observers complained that Charles wasn't really country, despite his obvious importance to the genre. Ultimately, Charles delivered a number 1 single when he teamed with Willie Nelson, another ex-Atlantic artist, to record "Seven Spanish Angels."

Nelson Larkin, who produced Royal's Atlantic America hits, was positioned as the A&R chief for Atlantic in the early days of the label, with as much power as Blackburn in the decision-making process. The marriage did not particularly work. In their first two years, about all Atlantic had to show for itself was one Royal hit, "Till I Can't Take It Anymore," and Robin Lee's minor hit remake of "Black Velvet," a major pop record for Atlantic's Alannah Myles.

In a 1991 reorganization, Blackburn received the controlling voice and Larkin departed. Atlantic achieved a stronger focus and almost immediately began seeing dividends with the emergence of Tracy Lawrence and John Michael Montgomery. Lawrence provided a strong, unique voice that leaned heavily on traditional country, while Montgomery became one of the premier balladeers of the 1990s, with songs such as "I Love the Way You Love Me," "I Swear," and "I Can Love You Like That." The latter two also became pop hits for Atlantic when the harmony-based All-4-One recorded them.

Atlantic stuck with Neal McCoy, a Filipino singer with an average voice but strong stage skills, for several years before he finally broke open with 1994's "No Doubt about It." A series of quasi-novelty records kept him almost constantly charted, and in 1998 the fans demonstrated their fondness for him by naming McCoy entertainer of the year in the TNN/*Music City News* awards.

Atlantic also managed four hits out of Confederate Railroad, a southern rock-driven group that dressed primarily in black and affected a tough stage image, countered by the philosophical nature of "Daddy Never Was the Cadillac Kind" and the tongue-in-cheek attitude of "Trashy Women."

Atlantic maintains a boutique philosophy, with the roster hovering around seven acts at all times. The staff has never wavered from fifteen to seventeen active staffers. The label is also strongly entrenched in research. Atlantic uses market studies to make most of its decisions about which singles are to be released to radio, drawing as much criticism as praise for that market-based philosophy.

Lynn Shults at Atlantic Records

In November 1994, I came on board Atlantic Records as vice president of media. I was to be responsible and accountable for all media activities.

First and foremost, I was responsible for the media activities of Tracy Lawrence, Neal McCoy, and John Michael Montgomery. My duties included the day-to-day positioning and imaging of the artist within the microcosm of country music, including the bookings of these artists on award shows, that is, CMA (Country Music Association), ACM (Academy of Country Music), and the Grammys. I was also responsible for booking our artists on late-night television appearances with Letterman, Leno, and so on.

I contacted personnel at major magazines in order to guarantee that our artists had feature stories in, and were on the covers of, magazines like *People* and *Country Music Weekly*; and I got coverage for our artists in the powerful trade magazines like *Billboard.*

The task of being vice president of media meant that a great deal of coordinating had to take place between the artist's personal staff, their independent publicist, and various other outside forces who would be directly or indirectly involved in the booking of the artist's events. Coordinating all of these people and events is not easily accomplished. There is a great deal of competition for prime-time exposure.

In many ways, my Atlantic years, from 1994 through December 1997, offered a good example of how observers, on the outside and on the inside of the industry, formed misconceptions regarding the exposure of the artists. From an outsider's perspective, to all of a sudden be a successful artist—one selling millions of records, being nominated for multiple awards, and having thousands of enthusiastic fans wanting to get near the artist—would appear to be one of the most euphoric experiences that could happen to an artist. What is not known, except by those people directly involved in the midst of such a frenzy, are the incredible pressures that fall on the artist at such times. It is impossible to meet everyone's demands and wishes. This type of stress and strain can take an artist to the very edge of an emotional breakdown. A balance must be found, and the artist must be prepared to tell many, many people no. There are just not enough hours in the day for the artist to meet all the demands being made on him.

From inside the industry, there are those who push their artist to accept and take advantage of every opportunity presented to him (especially booking agents, managers, and label executives). They squeeze everything out of his career in as short a period of time as possible because there is no guarantee as to how long an artist can operate at his peak. The quest for the industry brokers is for the artist to gross as much money as possible, even at the expense of the artist's emotional well-being.

Over the years it has been fascinating to sit in the middle of this feeding frenzy. What I have observed is that each artist is very different as to their appetites for stardom. I have seen many think that stardom was what they had wanted, only to find out that they really did not have the appetite for the demands and discipline required to negotiate the day-to-day life of a superstar.

Three Great Stars

The Atlantic roster is an interesting study in that John Michael Montgomery and Tracy Lawrence came out of nowhere and immediately achieved overnight superstardom. Neal McCoy was on a much slower track.

John Michael Montgomery

John Michael was living in his home town of Lexington, Kentucky, and had worked at various jobs, from being a waiter to sacking groceries to working in a liquor store. The entire time John worked his day gigs, he played his music at area clubs. He had his eye on Nashville, but because of an unpleasant experience his father had in Nashville, he was wary of the music business. John's dad had been taken by some con artists in Nashville, making John Michael somewhat skeptical of Nashville's music industry. [Some "sharks" reel aspiring young artists into their small, rented studios with worthless promises of fame and fortune. They take their money for recording a few songs, and then they tell them that, although they tried their best, no one was interested in them. The young artists leave Nashville with empty pockets and a disappearing dream.]

John's was a rags-to-riches story. He never pounded the streets on Music Row to try to get a label deal, a songwriter deal, or any other kind of deal, as 95 percent of all wanna-be artists do. John did nothing to try to sell himself. He just lived a normal life in Lexington, playing the clubs at night and working during the day.

One night, Estell Sowards, a guy who was looking for that one-in-a-million talent who could draw him into the mainstream music industry, wandered into a club where John was performing and thought, "God, this kid is great. I can make him a star." Even though John was reluctant, he gave Sowards the chance to see if he could find someone interested in him, and Soward's efforts eventually led to John Michael being signed to Atlantic Records.

Once John got his deal at Atlantic, one would think that everything would have been smooth sailing, but this was not the case. John faced a significant fork in the road while recording his first album. John knew that having a major label deal was a great opportunity for him, but he also realized that things were not going as well as they should be in the studio. John faced the dilemma of having to shut up and finish the album as it was or to stand up for what his intuition was screaming at him, which was, "This is not good enough."

John did what was right for him. He picked up the phone and called Rick Blackburn, who was president of Atlantic/Nashville, and expressed his feelings that the album had to be better. To Rick's credit, he listened to John and in the end agreed with him. The outcome of the meeting between John and Rick was to bring Doug Johnson [president of Giant Records as of 1998], an independent producer, into the studio. By doing so, John and Rick created the opportunity for John to achieve success beyond his wildest dreams, as Doug was an excellent producer.

John's first single release "Life's a Dance," debuted in *Billboard* magazine's country charts on October 3, 1992. From that moment on, John has been a superstar.

Tracy Lawrence

Tracy Lawrence, on the other hand, came to Nashville with the sole desire to be a star. He had no money, no contacts, and no idea how he was going to get into the doors. Tracy just had an unstoppable blind faith and belief in himself.

Tracy was discovered by accident. An Atlantic employee, Elroy Kahunek, who at that time was Atlantic's national promotion director, had gone to a small club outside of Nashville to see another aspiring artist, and Tracy was on the bill. The artist whom Kahunek had gone to see didn't inspire him at all, but Tracy Lawrence got Kahunek's attention. Lawrence was signed to Atlantic by Rick Blackburn, and the rest is history.

Neal McCoy

Neal McCoy, as opposed to John Michael and Tracy, was living in Longview, Texas, and like most aspiring artists, he had many different day gigs. But in Neal's case, his favorite thing to do was to be singing somewhere at every opportunity that presented itself.

Eventually Neal was brought to the attention of country music legend and Country Music Hall of Fame member Charley Pride. Neal is one of the most dynamic performers I have ever seen, and obviously Charley Pride recognized this quality in Neal and took him under his wing. Charley's interest in Neal lead to McCoy becoming his opening act in the late 1980s.

Charley spoke to every major label executive in Nashville about Neal but couldn't find a home for him. Label executives who had seen Neal perform live knew that they had seen a great entertainer, but no one knew how to package Neal and bring him into the country format.

Neal's problem, strange as it seems, is that he was too talented. Unlike most country entertainers, who just stand in one spot in front of the mike and sing, Neal McCoy was about being a total entertainer. He could cover a wide range of songs, from country standards through the repertoire of Frank Sinatra. He has incredible timing as he moves effortlessly from one side of the stage to the other, and his considerable natural instincts direct him, at any given moment, on how to elicit a response from the audience. Once again, it was Rick Blackburn who gave Neal a chance.

John Michael and Tracy hit with their first singles, while Neal struggled to find his niche. When everyone else was on tour in star buses, Neal and his band were traveling around the country in a Winnebago. Neal's first single on Atlantic debuted in the *Billboard* country charts in 1991, and as of February 1998 he is still trying to reach the upper pinnacle of superstardom.

Calling It a Day

During my years at Atlantic Records, from 1994 to 1997, one of the things that was reinforced in my mind was that no matter how hard some people may try to make someone else a star, sometimes it just doesn't happen.

People who become stars or superstars have something within them that is intangible, that ultimately connects them with the customer. Every label executive, every manager, every producer, and all others involved in the process of an artist being signed through being exposed to the public, are no more than facilitators. Granted, some are better than others, but we, as facilitators, can only create as positive and as healthy an environment for an artist as we can; the rest is up to that unknown intangible that makes superstars. There are hundreds of different ingredients in the recipe of success, and the recipe is different for each artist.

I am currently the president of Hayes Street Music Publishing Company, one of the few independent publishing companies left in Nashville. All of the large publishing houses, like Sony/Tree, BMG, and Warner/Chappell, are closely tied to their respective labels. Hayes Street is, and I say this with utmost sincerity, a well-known, highly visible, and totally reputable company. I couldn't be more pleased than to be in my current position at Hayes Street.

Life is about looking down new and unknown roads, and I know that a lot of wonderful things are possible for me as well as for all others who "Dare to dream!"

Lynn Shults

Growing Up

I was born in Old Hickory, Tennessee, a small community about ten miles east of Nashville, on October 19, 1944. My earliest memories of music stem from my mother, Delores, whose nickname was Fritzie. The radio was always on in our home, and my mother loved music and loved to dance. She used to hold me in her arms when I was a toddler and dance around the house with me. I'm a big believer in imprinting; things that you are exposed to when you are a small child leave their imprint on you as you mature and, in great part, have a definite influence on your life.

My first year of school was at Summertown Elementary School, which was in a small rural community in Lawrence County, Tennessee. Both of my parents were from that area. From the second grade through high school, I attended school in Gallatin, Tennessee, a town approximately thirty miles north of Nashville.

During my school years, I was far more interested in sports than I was in playing music. However, I had some friends who were interested in music and were attempting to teach themselves guitar. I always liked drums, so I began banging around on tin cans and glasses with a wooden spoon from the kitchen. Eventually, I learned to play drums and bass fairly well, but I never saw myself as a musician. Now I wish my mom had held a gun to my head and forced me to learn the piano, but that didn't happen.

When I graduated from high school, I went to Middle Tennessee State University in Murfreesboro and majored in business administration. I didn't graduate because in the middle of my freshman year I had to drop out when I came down with mononucleosis. Also at that time, my father was becoming extremely ill from cirrhosis of the liver from his long-term problem with alcoholism. In the middle of this family trauma, after I had recovered from mononucleosis, I left home and joined the Air Force. This was in 1963, and I was eighteen years old.

In less than a year, I received the sad news that my father had died, so I went home to my father's funeral. When I returned to my post, my sergeant knew that my mom was all alone and needed me; since it was still peacetime, he told me he would give me an honorable discharge for hardship reasons. I thought about it for a few days because I would not receive any military benefits because I hadn't completed my term of duty; however, I decided to go home to help my mom.

We were still living in Gallatin when I came home. I returned to the university and began work at WHIN Radio in Gallatin. I worked a split shift at the station as morning and afternoon disk jockey. The guys I had started playing music with in high school had evolved into a band. I didn't become part of the band because I had no time between work and school, but I became the band's unofficial manager. We rented various establishments where the band could play, like the National Guard Armory. We rented it for $50 a night and charged a buck a head admission. After the gig, we'd split the money taken in at the door, or, as it is called in music jargon, we'd take the gate. Eventually, we had a little circuit of venues where they played. The band was called the Deltas.

I continued to unofficially manage the band and work at the radio station until I went to work for Acuff-Rose Publishing Company. A good friend of mine, Norro Wilson, was instrumental in getting me the job at Acuff-Rose. Norro was from Scottsville, Kentucky. I don't know how Norro worked his way into the Nashville music industry, but he got a recording contract and later became an entertainer in Las Vegas. One day Norro came by the radio station and handed me a record of one of his recordings, which I liked a lot. From that point, Norro and I became good friends. Eventually, Norro introduced me to Bob McCluskey, who was general manager at Acuff-Rose. In 1965, when I was twenty-one years old, Bob asked me to come to work for Acuff-Rose in their promotion department. I quit the radio station, once again quit the university, and went to work for Acuff-Rose in November 1965.

Acuff-Rose

Fred Rose was a well-known professional piano player in Chicago when he decided to move to Nashville. He was, on his arrival, one of the most renowned keyboard players in town. Once here, he, along with Owen Bradley and others who were a part of the early Nashville music industry, put some bands together and played live music on WSM radio and other Nashville radio stations that aired nationwide.

Roy Acuff had major recordings out and was well known. Roy and Fred had gotten to know each other and became friends. The story goes that one day Roy Acuff walked into the office of Fred Rose and said, "Fred, we're starting a publishing company together. Here's $50,000; this ought to get us started." Fred said, "No, I don't want to do that. I don't think I can do that." Roy said, "Yes you can. Here's $50,000; so let's just start our company." That is how Acuff-Rose first began.

The story goes on to relate that the $50,000 was never needed. There was plenty of money already being generated through royalty payments on songs that Fred had written, the live radio shows he performed, and the session work he was doing. Roy, along with having saved more than the $50,000 he had offered Fred, was taking in a great deal of money via his recording contract, movies, and personal appearances.

Eventually, Hank Williams, Red Stewart, Boudleaux and Felice Bryant, Don Gibson, Pee Wee King, John D. Laudermilk, the Everly Brothers, Roy Orbison, and many other fine writers joined Acuff-Rose as staff writers.

Wesley Rose, Fred Rose's son, had been an accountant for the Gulf Oil Company in Chicago. When Fred passed away, Wesley moved to Nashville and began running his father's business. In later years, Wesley would be inducted into the Country Music Hall of Fame.

In 1965, when I came on board, Wesley was running the company. I never knew Fred. Acuff-Rose wasn't just a publishing company; it housed several different companies under its umbrella: publishing, management, booking, production, and Hickory Records, its in-house record label. Sue Thompson and the New Beats were on Hickory Records. Wesley was managing Roy Orbison, who was already a big star. The publishing company had some of the best writers in the country turning out the songs, and it handled the hit-song catalog of Hank Williams.

I was hired to be a national promotion director. Acuff-Rose, at that time, was the only Nashville-based publishing company that had a full staff. There were five of us on the promotion staff. We would get in our cars or hop on airplanes, depending on where we were headed, and travel to different places in the United States to call on radio stations to sell our product. We didn't just call on country radio stations; we called on stations that played all types of music because Acuff-Rose had artists from all genres of music recording the publishing companies' songs. It was one of the most successful publishing companies in North America and in some parts of Europe because Roy Orbison was very popular overseas. In 1967, Acuff-Rose had ten singles on the *Billboard* pop charts. We also had black artists recording our songs, so we were contacting R&B radio stations as well. Many songs from Acuff-Rose were recorded by artists on different labels.

Pop hits generated a great deal of money, sometimes more than $100,000, before they spiraled out and new songs hit the charts. Songs usually charted from twelve to twenty weeks on the *Billboard* singles charts from their debut to dropping off the charts. If you had a hit song that becomes a standard—a song recorded by many artists in all formats of music and recognized by the general public—then untold amounts of money were made.

Over an incremental period of time, checks from ASCAP, BMI, and SESAC would come into the company, upward of a quarter of a million dollars. ASCAP, BMI, and SESAC are performing rights organizations that collect money on behalf of the writers and publishers from all of the big national radio stations. They also collect worldwide from their foreign counterparts. The checks are split according to how many writers and how many publishers are involved with the particular song. If there is one writer and one publisher, the checks are split on a fifty-fifty basis; if there are three-writers and two publishers, the writers split 50 percent of 100 percent three ways, the publishers split 50 percent of 100 percent two ways, and so on. Today, if you look at the *Billboard* charts, one song may be split by several writers and publishers. Back then there was usually a fifty-fifty split. [A few years ago, Carey O'Neill wrote an article called "Where Does the Money Go," in *Music Row* magazine that still holds true today. The article gives a detailed breakdown of who gets what piece of the pie.]

Today there is an electronic detection system available to the performing rights organizations, but they don't choose to use it. The system is called BDS (Broadcast Data Systems), which can track exactly what songs are being played on a given number of radio stations; then, by multiplying out how many radio stations are in a particular format (that is, R&B, country, jazz, pop, and so on), you can get within 95 percent of actual plays on performance. I think that SESAC uses this system to track its Latin formats. I don't know what it uses in other formats. Since the performing rights organizations don't use this system, the only ones who understand their payment systems are the ones who make up the rules.

Performance payments are based on gross impressions, or the number of people listening to radio at a particular time, which is determined by Arbitron—a fairly accurate system. Only the top radio stations that report airplay lists to *Billboard* and *R&R* (*Radio & Record*) and the top 100 ADI (areas of dominant influence) markets are tracked. This is for the domestic United States. There are many different counterparts of performing rights organizations throughout the world. Each payment-gathering system is based on a different criterion; that is why there are companies like the Harry Fox Agency and CMI (Copyright Management, Inc.), which function as worldwide collection agencies for the publishers, who in turn pay the writer's portion out of their checks for both foreign and domestic airplay.

Anyway, I went to radio stations promoting our products. I promoted anything and everything that was under the Acuff-Rose umbrella: writers, songs, artists, and so on. I wined and dined the radio executives and their wives. Although payola has been around since time began, we weren't paying any radio stations to play our products.

I was promoting everyone from Andy Williams, who was signed to Columbia, to Kenny Rogers and the First Edition's big single "Just

Dropped in to See What Condition My Condition Was In," written by the legendary Mickey Newberry, who was a staff writer at Acuff-Rose. Mickey came to Acuff-Rose via Houston, Texas. Mickey was already a seasoned musician and songwriter when he was discharged from military service. He approached his uncle, Jay Boyette, who kept his hand on the pulse of the Nashville music industry and had gotten to know many people in the industry, for advice. So Jay brought Mickey to Nashville and introduced him to Wesley, and Mickey was signed.

I was paid a salary of about $20,000 a year, good money for 1965; no commission were being paid at that time. I was paid a salary plus expenses.

My mentor, Mel Foree, was a man who influenced me more than anyone else. I met Mel during my tenure at Acuff-Rose. For the first six weeks I was with Acuff-Rose, Mel traveled with me and showed me the ropes. He taught me to have honor and respect for the songs, the songwriters, the hard-working people in radio, and others who worked in the music industry with integrity and honesty. I learned by observing how Mel handled situations and people. He's the one who got me started out on the right track.

Starday-King

In 1969, I left Acuff-Rose over a dispute about money. I felt that I had proven myself to be of more worth than I was being paid, but Wesley wanted to keep all his people on an evenly salaried playing field. I understood why Wesley wanted to run his company like that, but I felt as though I was delivering a lot more than some of the other guys. During our dispute, Jim Wilson offered me a position at one of the first mail-order record catalog businesses in the United States.

The King Record label had been headquartered out of Cincinnati and was owned by a man named Sid Nathan. When Sid died, Don Pierce bought King Records and brought the label to Nashville. He located the offices in a little building out on Dickerson Road. He hired Hal Neely as the general manager and Jim Wilson as the national sales manager, and Charlie Dick [Patsy Cline's husband] was his national promotion man. I was hired on as the assistant national sales manager.

So I went from going out on the road calling on radio stations for Acuff-Rose to being in sales for Starday-King. My duties at my new job were to call on one-stops and national record distributors nationwide. A one-stop is a subwholesaler; it's a business that functions in between the actual wholesaler and the retailer. One-stops primarily sell records to jukebox operators. The wholesalers were our distributor for different music markets across the United States. This period of time was the heyday for independent distributors. Today there are only a few independent distributors handling all genres of music.

I would telephone the one-stops and drive or fly to their locations to make sales presentations for them to buy our product. We were handling all markets—R&B, country, pop, and jazz. In the R&B market, we had James Brown signed to Starday-King. In the country market, we had Red Sovine's trucker records and a lot of product in between. It was wild. Here we were, a few white guys in the South, with James Brown on our label. A James Brown album would sell a million units back in those days.

We would manufacture our records at several different independent manufacturing plants because none of the plants were large enough, by themselves, to handle a James Brown release. A distributor bought product from us for $2 to $4 a unit [a record]. The retail stores would sell a record for $6.98. Record company profits are used to pay salaries to in-house administrators and salespeople and royalties to their artists. [Artists' royalty percentages are determined by the contract drawn up between the label and the artist. Back then, a good average for an artist to receive would be between 8 and 10 percent. Today artists get as much as 14 percent, and superstars get even more.]

Labels also pay mechanical royalties to the songwriters and publishers. As I previously mentioned, splits between songwriters and publishers are derived from how many writers and publishers are involved on each song. Performance royalties [radio airplay] are paid to the publishers and song-writers by one of the three performing rights organizations I mentioned earlier. A songwriter is affiliated with only one performing rights organi-zation, and publishers are affiliated with all three. The reason for this is because staff writers don't all belong to the same performing rights orga-nization; when a song is published, the publisher must draw up different publishing contracts for ASCAP, BMI, or SESAC writers.

Producers are paid a percentage of the net record sales generated by the artist they are producing, in those days between 2 and 4 percent. The artist's booking agency is paid 10 percent of the agreed price for a perfor-mance. The artist may also receive a percentage of gross ticket sales, but it is the promoter who must put up all the money and take all the risks.

Starday-King had two labels: Starday Records and King Records. James Brown was on King Records. King was primarily R&B and pop; however, when Sid Nathan had the label in Cincinnati, it had everything on it, James Brown to country. At one time, King Records had Hawkshaw Hawkins and Little Willie John, who recorded the original "Fever," one of the most sensual songs that has ever been recorded.

Shelby Singleton

I worked for Starday-King until 1971, then I went to work for Shelby Sin-gleton at SSS International. [The initials SSS stood for Shelby's first, middle, and last names.] Shelby had been working for Mercury Records, but he and some Mercury executives had some kind of dispute. So Shelby moved to Nashville to start his own label, Plantation Records. Shelby brought his good friend Jerry Kennedy along with him when he moved to head up Mercury's Nashville office.

Jeannie C. Riley was signed to Shelby's Plantation Records, and soon after the magical wand of the gods was waved and "Harper Valley PTA" was born. Shelby had visions of grandeur that everything he touched would turn to gold, and for a while everything did. He also had a huge R&B act signed to his label, Johnny Taylor.

So he brought me in to pump up record sales at a salary of $25,000 a year, a new Cadillac, "and all you can steal from me." What Shelby meant by "all you can steal from me" was if I could get extra monies under the table and he didn't know about it, I could keep it. I had a big problem with this. I never got involved in the games a lot of the guys played, so my expense reports were relatively clean. Ever since there were three people on Earth and one wanted something out of another, payola's been around. I think payola has been grossly exaggerated in the music business. People who think that playing payola games will get you to the top are absolutely stupid. But a lot of people get caught up in the "who has" and the "who can control someone" by using money. I never did that. That's never been a part of how I do business.

Once again, I'm hawking those records—I'm on the phones, the airplanes, and the road. But I didn't work for Shelby very long.

Jack Clement

I worked for Jack "Cowboy" Clement in 1972. Jack owned this new little independent label, JMI, Jack Music Incorporated. In the drug-infused world surrounding Jack at the time, he formed JMI Records and the fictitious parent company Dipsy Doodle Construction Company. Jack felt there was no need for contracts between artists and labels; we were all among friends, and everyone was going to be treated fairly. It was under that premise that this great group of people came together in that moment of time, and history was made by these people who surrounded Jack.

The spiritual name of Jack's company was the Dipsy Doodle Construction Company; however, you won't find that name in any legal document. Those few of us in the know always knew that we were working for the Dipsy Doodle Construction Company under the auspices that this growing community of brilliant creative minds would make enough money to eventually embrace someone like Werner Von Braun, the renowned aerospace engineer, and have him build a space ship that would take all of us to Alpha Centauri. That was the mission of the Dipsy Doodle Construction Company. Hazardous, isn't it?

The movie wing of Jack's company is what eventually took Dipsy Doodle Construction down because it ate up a tremendous amount of resources. We didn't quite have enough money to build even one wing that this rocket ship required. As I recall, Cowboy did talk to Werner about it, at least on one occasion. The story goes: Jack picked up the phone and called the Huntsville Space Center in Huntsville, Alabama. They answered the phone, and Jack said, "Werner Von Braun, please." The next thing Jack knows, Werner is on the other end of the phone. It's one of those calls you make where you never dream you would actually reach the person you were calling. Even now, years later, just the thought of that happening makes us laugh.

In that great group of crazy people were Allen Reynolds, Dicky Lee, Bob McDill, Don Williams, Wayland Hollyfield, Chuck Neese, Charles Cochran, and Garth Fundis, who was the studio engineer. Everyone was doing something for Jack. Everyone would do a little bit of everything. Garth Fundis would sing; if you listen to Don Williams's version of that great record titled "Amanda," that real high background voice is Garth. Allen was a songwriter and a producer and definitely the money guy. He was the only one in the group who had any fiduciary responsibility.

Jack paid all of us a salary. We all came together, and it was a wonderful, brilliant time in my life, as crazy and out of control as it might have appeared to those on the outside. The excitement generated by this little band of Indians, this little independent record label, operating on our own, was phenomenal.

We put the first single out on Don Williams, who had been a part of Pozo-Seco singers, who had a huge hit on Columbia titled "Time." Don's first single with us was "The Shelter of Your Eyes," which was the first solo single Don ever put out. The song debuted December 16, 1972, and went to number 14 on the *Billboard* singles charts. We also recorded "Come Early Morning" for Don, which is a standard song for many, many folks. It went to number 12 on the *Billboard* singles charts. We cracked the Top 10 on the *Billboard* singles charts with a song recorded by Don titled "We Should Be Together," which went to number 5.

Eventually, Don Williams decided that the craziness at Jack's was not for him. Don didn't partake in the drugs and the other stuff that went on at Jack's at that time. Don was a very stable and well-balanced guy, and he had a family, so by moving on he did what was right for him.

Garth Brooks

One evening I was at the Blue Bird Cafe, and on this particular evening a guy named Garth Brooks was filling in for Ralph Murphy, a well-known songwriter and publisher in Nashville. Ralph couldn't make it for one reason or another, and when I heard Garth sing "If Tomorrow Never

Comes," it just hit me, in microseconds, that this guy was better than anybody we had on our label.

I always say that Ralph Murphy is the guy who should get the credit for
discovering Garth Brooks. If Ralph had been there that night, Garth would-
n't have been there, I wouldn't have heard him sing "If Tomorrow Never
Comes," and the career of Garth Brooks might never have happened.

Labels Give a Lot to Their Artists

What is given to the artists on a label is all you can give to any person in
this life: an opportunity. They're given an opportunity to fulfill a dream,
and if they are successful, the money will follow.

Artists are generally not given huge advances by the labels, and the
advances are recouped by the label when the artist starts making money.
The label picks up the huge tab for whatever is needed to facilitate that
artist, including paying for all of the studio time and paying the great session musicians, the songwriters, the publishers, the publicists, the photographers, the producers, and so on. There is only one way labels recoup the
money they spend on their artists, and that is from record sales.

Artists are never on salaries. However, they might be given draws from
time to time. If the artist needs money, the label executives decide whether
to advance funds to the artist. The executives decide whether the money
the artist is asking for is an honest request and whether the artist is trying
to bilk the label out of money.

Today, $750,000 to $1,000,000 is required to launch an artist. It costs a lot
of money to break an artist. The expenses include the producer's advance,
recording costs, videos, independent publicists, independent promoters,
marketing, and miscellaneous costs.

The budgets are put together by the individual departments, which then
meet collectively to discuss various strategies; however, the budgets are
approved by the president of the record label, and everyone involved in an
artist's career and receiving monies from the label's budget answers to the
respective department heads. The money allocated comes from the parent
company, whose home office is usually in New York or Los Angeles. As a
rule, the central accounting wing of the label is in charge of distributing and
signing checks. Contracts between the artist and the label determine what
monies are recoupable and what monies are not recoupable; for instance,
videos are usually recouped by the company on a fifty-fifty basis: half the
cost is charged back to the artist, and the label pays the other half.

The money is used in various ways, and there is no set percentage of
what monies go to what. Every contract is drawn up differently and negotiated differently; however, a very general breakdown of how the above
monies might be used is as follows:

1. Producers: Producers are advanced anywhere from $25,000 to $50,000. In the case of superstar artists, advances can be upward of $100,000. These advances are recouped against future album sales, which would equate to a royalty rate of between 2 and 4 percent, depending on the status of the producer and the recording artist.

Everything in this business "depends"—depends on wholesale value, depends on retail value. Contracts are written all over the ballpark, but, for instance, if the producer gets 4 percent, then the producer will be getting approximately 40¢ per album sold. So, for every million units sold, the producer will receive $400,000.

2. Recording costs: These include the following:

a. The session leader: The session leader receives a union scale of $645.38 for one three-hour session of studio time. If it takes eighteen hours, or six sessions to complete the tracking for a master session, this would equate to $6 \times $645.38 = $3,872.80$.

b. Each side musician (there are at least six side musicians on a master session): Each side musician receives a union scale of $330.52 for one three-hour session of studio time. If it takes eighteen hours, or six sessions to complete the tracking for a master session, this would equate to $330.52 \times$ 6 side musicians = $1,983.12 \times 6$ sessions = $11,898.72. The session leader and the side musicians would be paid, given our approximations, a total of $15,771.52, for tracking four or five days in the studio. The figure for musicians, engineers, and background vocalists can easily go to between $30,000 and $50,000 when engineering fees, overdubs, added instrumentation, and added background vocals are incorporated into our budget. The pay outlined here is basic. The vocal performance of the artist must also be considered in the recording costs. Those costs can vary greatly, depending on how many musicians and background vocalists are involved in the total process of recording the album.

c. The recording artist: If the artist is not an established artist, he may receive an advance against future album sales of between $25,000 and $50,000.

d. Studio rental: Rental rates range from the low side of $2,500 per day to the high side of $5,000 per day. On a thirty-day approximation, studio rental may be $100,000.

The musicians do not receive the total amount of money up front but are paid for each three-hour session they work. The total studio cost, including the producer's advance, to complete one album project is approximately $250,000. An album may take six months to one year to complete. Everyone is way too busy to do a project straight through with no breaks; therefore, the musicians, producers, engineers, background singers, and artist are in and out of the studio during this period of time, laying down the tracks and perfecting the project. If all the days were squeezed together, one month out of one year would be a good approximation of how long it takes to complete one album project.

3. Videos: These cost somewhere in the neighborhood of $225,000 for three videos, $75,000 per video, for the three single songs that are selected from the album to receive airplay and television exposure.

4. Publicists: These are hired as independent publicists who work along with the label's publicity team. The publicist's job is to get the artist exposed to the print and television media. An independent publicist will cost about $50,000 a year, which could be recoupable, half recoupable, or nonrecoupable, it all "depends." The in-house publicist as well as the independent publicist work together as part of the record label's and artist's team in getting the artist known through the print media and television, preparing press releases, deciding what photos are going to be used for media kits and putting those media kits together, and maintaining a national media list and specific media lists, including the names and addresses of all the people the media kit should be mailed to. These lists contain all of the names, addresses, and phone numbers of all of the major entertainment reviewers, all of the newspapers, and Burrell's collection service of worldwide press reviewers. The publicists must get the artist known to the public and connect the artist's name with that artist until his name becomes a household word. Publicists have their key sources, which are those people who the publicist can reach and influence the most for the benefit of the artist.

By now, we have paid out approximately $525,000 of our million, which leaves us $475,000.

5. The promotion department: This department will spend an enormous amount of money because of the size of the staff, which consists of a team of anywhere from ten to fifteen people, each of whom is receiving a salary anywhere from $60,000 to $80,000 a year, plus expenses. The salaries and expenses are not included in this budget, as they are normal costs of doing day-to-day business at the record label. The in-house promotion staff work with independent promotion people (in layman's terms, independent promoters could be equated to lobbyists in our political system) who are paid collectively, anywhere from $30,000 to $50,000, to promote the first single release off the album.

6. Marketing costs: These will be a minimum of $100,000 a month for three months, or $300,000. The label's marketing staff bring the attention of the new artist to the distribution system. The distribution system is the label's company-owned distribution wing as well as key retail and mass merchandisers involved in the process of selling recorded music. This process includes, but is not limited to, small mom-and-pop retail stores, national chain retail stores normally found in shopping malls, and your mass merchandisers who place the albums in K-Mart, Wal-Mart, Target, and so on.

The money discussed here is allocated for advertising in print, radio, and television and in securing key placement in the retail stores; that is, when you walk into a retail store and an album is staring you in the face, this is not an accident. The placement of the album has been bought and paid for by the record label.

7. *Miscellaneous:* The remaining $125,000 may be allocated by spending more money on miscellaneous marketing, promotion, and various increased advances. There are, of course, many more expenses than those previously noted, for instance, wardrobe, tour support, hotels/motels, personal management, road management, road musicians, bus drivers, security, photographers, equipment handlers, electricians, and sound personnel. At major labels, the label's presidents make $250,000 to about $1,000,000 a year, plus expenses. This figure consists of normal label operating costs that are not part of our budget; however, depending on their individual contracts, label presidents may or may not receive a percentage on album sales on top of their salaries and expenses.

Dividing the Pie

Normally, an artist will have a reduction clause from 12-$\frac{1}{2}$ percent to 20 percent, in his contract. This is called a package deduction. If it's 20 percent, an artist is being paid on 80 percent of 100 percent.

If an album retails for $15 and there are ten cuts [songs] on the album, 70¢ goes to the publishers, who then split the money with the songwriters. If there is one publisher and one writer, each publisher would receive 35¢ per album sale. If there are two publishers and one writer, each publisher would receive 17¢, and the writer would receive 35¢. If there are three publishers and three writers, the publishers receive 12¢, as do the three songwriters, give or take 2¢. These payments are referred to as mechanical payments, which are collected by the publishers and paid to the songwriters, as opposed to airplay payments, which are collected on behalf of the publishers and songwriters by ASCAP, BMI, or SESAC.

Distribution monies vary after the product is sold by the label to its distributors, depending on whether the distributors are pricing the product wholesale or retail. The labels always sell wholesale.

RCA Records might sell an album wholesale to WEA [Warner/Elektra/Asylum], Atlantic's distributors, for $8. Then WEA may sell it to Anderson or Handleman, the distributors for Wal-Mart and K-Mart, for $11 per album. Then Wal-Mart and K-Mart sell it for approximately $12.99 if the suggested retail price is $15 per album. There are many unknowns because many different deals are made as to how to price a product.

The label will receive approximately $3 gross profit per album sale, and out of that $3 the label has to absorb all of its general costs of day-to-day operations—telephone, lights, and salaries for a huge staff. So that $3 is not profit for the label but just recoupment for all of the costs.

The prices change according to units sold. Millions of albums have to be sold before profits are made.

The manufacturing costs will go down in relationship to units sold. As the pricing changes, so do the payments and recoupments to all of those involved. There are escalation clauses in artists' contracts, and there are a myriad of ways in which recoupment fees change for everyone involved with the project. Then, when the album is put on sale, all of the fees change again.

Producers

The monetary arrangement a label will have with an independent producer is determined by the reputation of the producer and the magnitude of the artist he wants to produce. An established artist sets the tempo for financial negotiations. An independent producer may be paid from $25,000 to $50,000 to produce the project. If the artist has already sold platinum [one million units sold], then the producer's advance may be much greater than $50,000.

Employment Security

There is no job security working at a major label. Working for a label is like many other industries today. Years ago, when you went to work for a company, you stayed with that company until you retired. Many companies were once owned by individuals, or the major shareholders were individuals, and most companies were built on loyalty between the employer and employee. People who worked for those companies stayed there until they retired. Many people, especially the baby boomer generation, were raised with those expectations.

In today's corporate climate, and not just in the record industry, the attitude is, "What did you do for me today, and what are you going to do for me tomorrow?" There seems to be a constant and continual wholesale reshuffling of employees with most large companies. It's extremely rare to find loyalty in any industry today. I also believe this type of turnover is unique to the American culture.

The president of a company used to really mean something. Today the presidencies are not as meaningful because the president may not actually run the company—you have a CEO and a CFO. And in some cases the president is just a front guy for the executives on the board of directors who really run the company. In rare instances there may be a president who is really a brilliant guy and the leader of the company. It varies, but most executives are on three-to-five-year contracts.

In Nashville's music industry, Joe Galante has been the senior for a long time. RCA is the only corporate company he's ever worked for. The other president who has been around for many years is Jim Ed Norman [president of Warner Bros. and Reprise Records]. With these two exceptions, executives are usually changed out every three to five years. The rapid turnover is one of the reasons that so much money is paid to executives—it's a high-profile, fast game. Either companies have hit artists or they don't. If they don't have hit artists, then certainly label executives are going to change.

Balance of Power

Normally there is a balance of power set up among the various departments in companies to prohibit one department from wielding too heavy a stick. However, one of the three is usually the strongest, and one of the three is the weakest. Whoever has the highest executive standing within the departments will have the most power. If an executive comes from an A&R background, the A&R department will be favored; if an executive comes from a promotion background, then that department will be favored.

Market Research

Market research is done by putting from forty to a hundred people in a room. Then the music from the artist's new album is intertwined with a lot of other music, and audience response is logged. It works a lot like television's Nielsen ratings. Some companies do market research prior to releasing the new singles, and others do not.

The percentage of the budget spent for marketing, promotion, and so on varies; there is no set percentage. If you have a hit record and think you have a hit artist, you will spend whatever it takes to deliver the product to the marketplace. Usually, more money is spent than is necessary. Sometimes as much as $20 million might be spent to promote and market a product that is believed in by the company.

Prior to an artist going out to various road venues, key radio people are contacted by the artist's management team and publicists in order to give the radio executives enough advance notice to ensure they're scheduling time for the artist. When an artist is sent out on the road, the mission is to introduce the artist to those people making decisions about what record and what artists will get played on their radio stations. Normally, the artist is one-on-one with the music director and the program director over lunch or dinner.

Highs and Lows

My years at Capitol were, in many ways, a lot of fun for me. I felt good about myself, and I felt as though the company was doing a great job. I got to work with a lot of great artists. However, in some ways, those years were extremely painful for me.

Capitol/North America is owned by EMI, a global corporate operation headquartered out of Los Angeles, California. The frustration for me was that, although I was technically running the label as vice president of A&R for ten years, we could never gain our independence from the parent company. They would never set us up as our own individual profit-and-loss center. It was kind of like a child always having to go ask a parent for permission to do something.

The CEO for Capitol/North America at that time was Bhaskar Menon, and his management style was to keep us dependent and reliant on his decisions. Although there were a lot of decisions we could make, when it came to major decisions, especially regarding money, it was having to ask for an allowance and explaining what it was needed for. This system isn't inherently wrong because someone always has to be accountable, but the problem was that we here in Nashville knew the country marketplace and the country arena; they didn't. A budget is just a guideline that is constantly being shifted, and Capitol under Bhaskar Menon was rigidly controlled; at least our offices were rigidly controlled by his budgets, and this was very frustrating for me.

I had brought Alabama into Capitol, and all we had to do to sign them was to guarantee them a release of an album, and the company would not do that. These years were the transition years, when artists were signed to "singles deals" and the company would put out a single or two or three; if a single didn't become a hit, then an album was never released. The thinking of many in the industry was, "If you're not willing to put out an album, then you're not committing very much to this artist. And if you're not going to commit, we're not going to commit." It was kind of like moving down the food chain, and it was very frustrating not to be allocated the budget to commit to our artists. So we didn't get to sign Alabama.

The other part of the business that was frustrating for me was that we were having a lot of success and generating a lot of money, but the money wasn't invested back into the Nashville operation. Although there have been changes, the policy of parent companies not reinvesting money back into the part of the company that made the money is really hard to deal with.

For instance, Atlantic Records was generating $50 million a year for a couple of years, which is a huge profit margin, through artists like John Michael Montgomery, Tracy Lawrence, and Neal McCoy. But Rick Blackburn doesn't want the company to grow; he wants to keep it at fifteen employees. So, with a company that small, where do all those profits go?

Rick's reasoning is not necessarily wrong about keeping a label small. Rick knows that he's doing. He was once the president of CBS/Nashville and had a staff of sixty or seventy people, but he prefers to operate with a small staff. Rather my frustration is with all of those huge profits going into Time Warner's New York corporate fund and not bouncing back to Nashville.

Luke Lewis

Mercury Records/Nashville

Courtesy of Dan Loftin

Physical strength is measured by what we can carry; spiritual by what we can bear.

—Anonymous

About Mercury Records

Mercury is an essential element in the production of thermometers; thus it should come as no surprise that Mercury, like most businesses, has run hot and cold during its more than fifty years in existence.

The label was established in the summer of 1945 by Chicago businessman Irving Green, who owned a record-pressing plant, and Berle Adams, the manager for Louis Jordan. Irving saw a sign advertising the new line of Mercury automobiles and decided to name his company the Mercury Radio and Television Corporation. Initially, Mercury developed itself as an R&B label, although within short order it was exploring the other realms of music, too. Tony Martin gained Mercury's first pop hit, "To Each His Own," in 1946, while Sheriff Tom Owen and His Cowboys recorded the first Mercury country record at the end of 1945.

On March 1, 1947, the firm officially became Mercury Records as four different companies merged. In the process, Mercury had its own pressing plant, its own distribution company, and even its own album jacket manufacturing plant.

That August, Mercury placed an executive in Nashville for the first time, appointing Les Hutchens to develop talent for the label in the home of the Grand Ole Opry. But Hutchens remained only a short while, leaving to manage Cowboy Copas. In his stead, Mercury appointed Murray Nash to head its country efforts out of Knoxville in March 1948. Nash brought on board such artists as Bill Carlisle, the Sons of the Soil (with a singer named Don Gibson), and Flatt and Scruggs, a then little-known duo that had just left the employ of bluegrass pioneer Bill Monroe. Though they stayed only a couple of years, Flatt and Scruggs recorded their classic "Foggy Mountain Breakdown" for Mercury.

Green tried to push Nash into relocating from Knoxville to New Orleans, but Nash refused. Instead, he resigned on April 1, 1951, allowing the company to hire Walter "D" Kilpatrick. In 1955, Kilpatrick was transferred to Chicago, where he stayed for a year before returning to Nashville to manage the Grand Ole Opry.

By late 1956, Mercury was well off the pace of the country market leaders RCA, Decca, and Columbia. Harold "Pappy" Daily and Don Pierce had developed a successful Texas-based label, Starday, which had launched the career of George Jones. Mercury persuaded the two to merge, creating Mercury-Starday and bringing Jones to the label's roster. That arrangement lasted only eighteen months, with Pierce and Daily parting ways. Daily, however, fed artists he was developing back to Mercury, bringing both The Big Bopper and Claude Gray to Mercury.

That arrangement, however, did not last long either. Art Talmadge, who headed Mercury's pop A&R department, left the label in 1960 to join the newly formed UA Records, and when he did, Daily left as well, with Jones departing to record for UA. Green turned to regional sales manager Shelby Singleton, who represented Mercury in Louisiana and asked him to run the label. Singleton moved to Nashville in January 1961. Two months later, his Shreveport associate, Jerry Kennedy, moved to Nashville as well.

That same year, Philips Electronics purchased Mercury and expanded the company to three labels: Mercury, Smash, and Philips. Singleton and Kennedy turned Mercury's Nashville operation into a stronghold almost immediately, scoring with such hits as Leroy Van Dyke's "Walk on By," Joe Dowell's "Wooden Heart," and Ray Stevens's "Ahab the Arab." Mercury began signing acts from other labels, acquiring Roy Drusky from Decca and Faron Young from Capitol. Jerry Lee Lewis, whose career had plummeted when the world discovered he'd married his young cousin, joined Smash Records in 1963. Roger Miller, who'd previously flopped on five different labels, signed with Smash when the label offered him $100 per side for sixteen recordings. Out of those sessions came "Dang Me" and "Chug-a-Lug," and Smash had suddenly turned Mercury into a hot property. Singleton left on top, forming his own companies in January 1967. The following year, he garnered one of the biggest hits of 1968, when Jeannie C. Riley recorded "Harper Valley PTA" for his Plantation Records. The dobro player on that recording was Jerry Kennedy, who assumed the direction of Mercury in the wake of Singleton's departure.

Kennedy was willing to take chances on talent. Lewis, for example, had not picked up in sales in the first five years of the Mercury contract. With the Killer's Smash tenure on the line, Kennedy talked him into a country session, and it led to a string of hits, including "Another Place, Another Time," "Chantilly Lace," and "What's Made Milwaukee Famous (Has Made a Loser Out Of Me)," that made Lewis one of the strongest country acts of the early 1970s.

Kennedy also signed Tom T. Hall, who had emerged as one of the era's top songwriters, to an unlikely deal that hinged on Hall's subtle story songs. Hall turned the deal into a winner, yielding such landmark hits as "I Love," "(Old Dogs, Children and) Watermelon Wine," and "The Year Clayton Delaney Died."

Hall and Bobby Bare, a Mercury labelmate for a scant two years, introduced Kennedy to Johnny Rodriguez, a Hispanic singer in his early twenties. Kennedy had once passed on Charley Pride, who became the genre's first successful African-American country singer, but he signed Rodriguez, who emerged as a rare Latino country star. It helped that he developed a following of teenage girls, attracted by his matinee looks, and it helped that he possessed a unique, edgy voice.

The signing that paid the longest dividends was the Statler Brothers. The Virginia-based quartet, hinging on gospel harmonies, hadn't had a hit since 1965's "Flowers on the Wall," but under Kennedy's production they developed a remarkable consistency that kept them making hit records until the late 1980s. Their popularity remained solid enough that in the 1990s, they hosted their own variety show on TNN.

In the midst of all that activity, the European PolyGram corporation bought Mercury in 1971, and nine years later the company's American operations center was moved from Chicago to New York.

In 1983, Frank Jones took over the leadership of Mercury, allowing Kennedy to head into independent production. Jones headed the company for two years, though his tenure was rather unremarkable. The only real success to emerge from his stay at Mercury was the June 1983 signing of Kathy Mattea, whose musical integrity and willingness to experiment brought her a number of CMA awards, undergirded by such successful singles as "Eighteen Wheels and a Dozen Roses" and "Where've You Been."

Steve Popovich, whose career had intersected with Michael Jackson, B. J. Thomas, and Meat Loaf, replaced Jones. Because of eclectic tastes he signed polka artists, rough-hewn David Lynn Jones, and past-their-commercial-prime acts Johnny Cash and Johnny Paycheck, who did not improve Mercury's position.

In December 1987, promotion man Paul Lucks took over the company, and ten months later record producer Harold Shedd joined the label. Shedd had produced Alabama's hits for the first eight years of their existence and had brought K. T. Oslin to RCA. Both of those acts had gone against the grain in finding success, and Shedd hoped to continue finding left-field diamonds for Mercury.

His first signing was the Kentucky HeadHunters, a backwoods group with a rock 'n roll flair that turned Nashville on its ear. Its heavy guitars and penchant for traditional country lyrics netted two CMA awards for vocal group of the year, and the band set a precedent for the rockin' country movement that would grip Nashville in the 1990s.

Shedd also signed Billy Ray Cyrus, who had developed a huge club following in Kentucky and West Virginia with a brand of country that, like the HeadHunters, relied heavily on a rock feel. Cyrus also mixed in a certain sexuality, and when he crossed paths with "Achy Breaky Heart" he earned sales of nine million albums as well as one of the biggest backlashes ever witnessed in Nashville.

Former MCA executive Luke Lewis moved from Los Angeles in 1992 to oversee the Nashville office, and under his leadership both Sammy Kershaw and Toby Keith became very successful. Shania Twain, whom Shedd had signed, retooled her music after marrying rock producer Mutt Lange and reinvented her image, mixing smoldering sexuality with a certain girl-next-door attitude. *The Woman in Me* became the biggest selling country album ever recorded by a female.

Shedd moved over to Polydor when Mercury established a sister label in 1994. A&M, distributed by Mercury, took over the label in the spring of 1996, but just after Labor Day 1998 the Nashville office was shut down. Keith, who had joined the Polydor/A&M roster in the shuffle, returned to Mercury, while the rest of the roster was released. Chely Wright, who had won an award from the Academy of Country Music, signed with MCA, where she showed increased chart activity in 1997.

Like Wright, the entire Mercury operation was set to join MCA at the end of 1998. MCA's purchase of Polygram had not been entirely settled, but it appeared that both the Mercury and the MCA label would survive.

Luke Lewis

Early Years

I was born in Philadelphia on January 2, 1947. My dad was in the real estate business. He opened an office in Florida, and we moved to West Palm Beach when I was three years old. I went to a private school in Jacksonville, Florida, when I was sixteen years old. While there, I became friends with a guy named Gram Parsons. [Gram Parsons is credited with being the father of country rock music.] I always had an interest in music. I used to hang around our local record stores and listen to music. I love music; I like all kinds of music, and there is no particular genre I prefer, as long as it is good music.

I grew up as a 1960s baby-boomer. Like a lot of people, I was influenced by R&B, the Rolling Stones, and the Beatles. I probably took a bit of a turn in my listening habits because of my friendship with Parsons toward the Byrds, the Flying Burrito Brothers, and country music.

Later, I went to college in Ithaca, New York. I stayed in school for a couple of years, then I dropped out and was drafted into the Army in 1967. I worked as a journalist while I was in the Army and was sent to Fort Campbell, Kentucky, which is right on the Tennessee border. I used to hang around the camp library to read and listen to all kinds of music. I met a woman in the library named Betsy, who was to become my wife in 1970.

After I was married, we moved around a bit. We moved back to Florida, where I worked in the restaurant business for a few years. I did all kinds of things. I was a car mechanic, a welder, a painter, and a bartender. We just kind of bounced around for a few years and finally wound up back in Tennessee, where I went back to college in Clarksville, where Betsy had graduated. I worked in a record store while attending classes.

I had a friend who worked for a record distributor in Memphis, who told me there was a job opening stocking records in records stores around the Southeast. I took the job, and they gave me a car and $125 a week. I stayed with that job for a couple of years, then I worked for a rack jobber. I was constantly coming to Nashville because of my business. Whenever I was in Nashville, I began knocking on doors trying to get a job at a record company. I had no idea what I wanted to do; I just knew that I wanted to be around the music industry. I also knew that my talents lay in the business end of the business, not the creative end. I loved music but wasn't a very good musician or writer; so that left the business end open to me.

Eventually, I went to work for a now-defunct trade magazine called *Record World*. I was hired as the southeastern editor in 1976. I worked there for about a year. I took the opportunity to explore the music industry to find out what I really wanted to do in music.

I befriended Joe Galante, president of RCA Records, and Rick Blackburn, president of CBS Records, Nashville. David Conrad was working for Pi-Jem Publishing Company, Tim Wipperman worked at Warner Bros. Music, and David Hogan was making videos. [Joe Galante is currently the president of RLG/Nashville, Rick Blackburn is the president of Atlantic records, David Conrad is head of Almo Irving Publishing Company, Tim Wipperman is the head of Warner Bros. Publishing Company, and David Hogan, through making his videos, gained legendary status by filming Sheryl Crow and Melissa Etheridge.]

Anyway, the bunch of us were young turks back then. Joe Galante, who had moved to Nashville from New York, had a pretty big influence on me because he was in the marketing end of the business. Joe inspired me by convincing me that a person didn't have to be in the creative end of things to make a living at a record company if he was a good record person.

I wanted to stay in Nashville. I liked living here, my wife's from here, I like the music here, and I liked the idea of working for a small label that was affiliated with a major distribution company. So I decided to learn all I could and took a job as a sales representative for CBS. I worked out of their Atlanta and Memphis offices covering the southeast region. In 1979, the company moved me to Dallas, Texas, to be a sales manager for the southwest territory. Then I moved to New England, where I headed up their northeast division for six years. All this time, I sort of had my hand up, saying, "I want to go back to Nashville." However, that opportunity had not yet arrived.

I had a mentor, Al Teller, who was the president of CBS. In 1989, Al went to work for MCA in Los Angeles, California. Al encouraged me to move to California, so I did, and I worked as head of sales and marketing for MCA for four years.

Mercury Records

My dream of living and working in Nashville was alive for a long time before I finally went to work for Mercury Records/Nashville as president in 1992.

Mercury Records is owned by Polygram, which is a publicly traded company. Most of the stock in Polygram is owned by Philips Electronics, which is a Dutch company. Polygram also owns Island Records, A&M Records, Motown Records, Mercury Records, Deutsch-Gramophone [a classical division], Verve Records, and various other labels around the world. Polygram is a huge international company. Mercury/Nashville has always been autonomous, although I report to Danny Goldberg, who runs the Mercury Records Group.

In 1992, when I walked in the door as president of Mercury/Nashville, Billy Ray Cyrus's "Achy Breaky Heart" was a huge record. As of 1998, Billy Ray is still on Mercury and was soon to release a new record, but "Achy Breaky Heart" was the biggest-selling debut record in the history of the music industry; since then, Hootie and the Blowfish and Alanis Morisette have eclipsed Billy's sales record. "Achy Breaky" was gold when I arrived at Mercury and eventually sold in excess of thirteen million records.

The Labels

Some of the records I put out as the new president were the first releases for Shania Twain and Toby Keith.

I brought Keith Stegall, a great songwriter and producer, on board to help with creative decisions. Keith recently had two songs in the Top 10 *Billboard* country charts, and he received a Grammy nomination for producing Alan Jackson's album *Everything I Love*. He also produced Alan's chart topper "Between the Devil and Me." Keith produced and cowrote the number 1 single in the nation, "Love of My Life," for Sammy Kershaw, and he was instrumental in getting Terri Clark signed to Mercury.

As of March 1998, we have eighteen artists on our roster. Mercury is as big as RCA; however, RCA also has BNA (Berry Field Nashville Airport) Records under its umbrella; MCA has MCA Records and Decca Records; and Sony has Epic, Lucky Dog, Columbia, and Monument Records. Therefore, those labels have many artist rosters for their different label divisions, but Mercury has only one country label. I think we have a proportionate roster to the other major labels, given our single-label status.

At Mercury we have various departments. Our sales, marketing, and promotion departments are run by John Grady; our communications department, run by Sandy Neese, handles press and publicity; the head of our creative department, Jim Kemp, oversees the artwork, photographs, and album cover artwork; Retta Harvey heads up our video production department; Keith Stegall heads up our A&R department; and our head of finance and operations is Ken Robold. We have forty people at the label. The department heads report to me to discuss any important decisions that need to be made.

There are some really difficult decisions that have to be made that have an enormous impact on the bottom line. Some of these decisions involve who you sign or who you drop or which single you're going to release and which one you're not going to release, and so many of these decisions are subjective. Somebody ultimately has to make the call, and it doesn't seem to work in a committee. I certainly take input from everybody. Sometimes I joke with the people I work with and say, "Everyone here gets to have an opinion, but you don't get a vote."

The Artists

The stars lined up when we signed Shania to the label. After her first record, which sold about 120,000 units, she met and married Mutt Lange, a legendary rock 'n roll producer and songwriter. Shania and Mutt made her second record together. They wrote the material and produced the session. The album titled *The Woman in Me* sold in excess of ten million units. This was the biggest-selling record by a female in the history of country music. In 1997, Shania's sales surpassed those of Patsy Cline. In 1998, we released her third album, which has sold four million units internationally and still counting.

Terri Clark, like Shania, is from Canada. Terri's first album went platinum and her second went gold. Her third album was released in 1998. Sammy Kershaw has several gold and platinum albums and is currently enjoying his biggest success with his sixth album, *Labor of Love*. The first single, which was number 1 in the *Billboard* country singles charts, is titled "Love of My Life." The album is now gold. In 1997, we released John Anderson's album. We're very proud to have John on our label. He's one of the best singers in the business. He's really a cool guy. Toby Keith has had several gold and platinum records, and in 1998 we released *Dream Walkin,'* which is almost at gold status in units sold. Kathy Mattea has been on the label longer than our other artists. She's been signed to Mercury for thirteen years, as of 1998. She is currently working on her next album release. Kathy has had an incredible career. She has enormous integrity and makes beautiful music. In 1998, Mark Wills completed his second album, titled *Wish You Were Here.* Kim Riche, one of our singer/songwriters, has written some huge country hits for other artists. One song Kim wrote, titled "Believe Me Baby I Lied," was a monstrous hit for Trisha Yearwood.

One of the coolest things about Mercury Records is its back catalog of albums. We have all of Hank Williams's recordings, a lot of Roger Miller's music, and a very big catalog on Tom T. Hall, who continues to record new music for us. Hank Williams was on MGM Records, and years ago Polygram, our parent company, bought Hank's entire catalog. We also own some Johnny Cash and George Jones recordings.

New York

Our home office is in New York; however, Mercury/Nashville works from its own profit-and-loss statements. We are a very autonomous label, and most of the money we bring into the label is reintegrated into our label's projects. Also, we have a good deal of support from Polygram Group Distribution, our distributor.

We currently have a record out on Shania that is crossing over into the pop market, so the Mercury/New York staff works the pop radio stations for us. We are also supported by their press department in New York. They have some leverage that we don't have, so that helps us out, too. It's basically a pretty nice working relationship because we have access to New York's resources whenever we need them.

Danny Goldberg, Mercury's president and CEO, and I have similar backgrounds as journalists. He's a wonderful guy. Not only does he not interfere, but he adds his support to the label whenever appropriate. Danny came into the business as a manager for Bonnie Raitt and Nirvana. He's a music person. He came into his position in New York after I had been in Nashville for a while, and we were fortunate enough to have a profitable operation. So Danny's not inclined to give me a lot of direction, but he does give me a lot of support.

Signing Artists

We have a few scouts who work for us looking for potential new artists. And the publishing community in Nashville has a history of developing artists as singer/songwriters, so we have contacts in the publishing community. From time to time they bring their artists to the attention of the label executives for possible consideration. Dick Frank, a Nashville attorney, brought Shania to Norro Wilson, a record producer, who then brought Shania to Mercury Records. Norro made the first demos on Shania, which resulted in her being signed to Mercury.

There are regular showcase spots in Nashville where artists perform and invite various label people to come out and listen to them. Some people get signed through showcasing. It's like any other business—it's who you know. Sometimes it's very difficult for someone who is trying to be an artist to get to any of us; however, I believe that if they have what it's going to take to be a successful artist, then they will also have the ingenuity to figure out how to get to us.

I have never seen anyone signed to a label overnight. It's a long, hard, fiercely competitive process, and very few make it to the majors. A lot of dues are paid along the way. My definition of paying dues is no more and no less than learning all of the ins and outs of the business and, of course, not getting an attitude along the way. No one wants to sign anyone who needs an attitude adjustment.

Shania, Billy Ray, Kershaw, and Toby—just about every artist on this label and just about all successful artists—pay enormous dues before they get a break. They may play around town for years and years and get to know key people before they are ever considered by the majors. I can't remember anyone ever becoming a star overnight. Even LeAnn Rimes has been singing since she was a baby. It's not easy. You certainly need some luck to get into a position to have the opportunity to be signed.

A few male artists were signed as they were approaching thirty, but that's about the age limit. People in their forties or fifties have little, if any, hope of being signed to a major label. Music is a young person's business because the most active record buyers are young people. Country radio targets the age of their listening audience between twenty-five and fifty-four years of age. That allows for a lot of latitude; however, any artist who has had meaningful success has sold a lot of records to people under the age of twenty-five, as they're the buyers as well as the listeners. Radio is the main media we use to give our artists exposure. It's targeted to an older audience than the majority of those who buy CDs—the teenagers who listen for hours in their rooms.

The Money

The cost to make an average record in Nashville is around $150,000. This cost does not include marketing, promotion, advertising, and so on. Between $20,000 and $40,000 of $150,000 goes to the producer. The rest goes into studio time, session musicians, engineers, background vocalists, cartage fees, mix time, and extra equipment fees. The average cost for a music video is $70,000. Many record labels hire outside publicity people. We have a four-person in-house staff who handle most of our publicity.

Producers, and sometimes A&R people, have made arrangements wherein they receive a point, which is a percentage of album sales, from artists whom they have gotten signed to the label. Some label executives have deals wherein their bonuses are predicated on profits from record sales as opposed to the gross. This plan encourages the label to make money prior to payouts.

Entry-level positions in the music industry pay next to nothing. A person coming in to work in the mail room would start at between $15,000 and $20,000 a year. However, there are people on staff who are making as much as $200,000 a year if they have been around a long time or are heading up one of the label's departments.

Although Nashville is the friendliest town I've ever lived in, in terms of executives, artists, writers, and musicians hanging out together, when the time comes to compete in the marketplace, no holds are barred—the music

industry is fiercely competitive. I say it's just good old American capital-
ism, free enterprise at work.

Growth

In the 1970s, when I got into the music business, the entire industry was in
a growth phase. But, like our economy, eventually the music industry fell
to pieces in the early 1980s; there were enormous layoffs, and everybody
was downsizing.

In 1981, the CD came into the marketplace, and that rejuvenated the
entire industry because we were able to sell products we had previously
sold on LPs. New musical trends also came along at that time, and the
music industry was invigorated and healthy. Then, in the mid-1980s, the
industry hit a slump because the music was not impacting the listeners. It
sounded like a mix between adult contemporary and easy listening. It just
wasn't country. In 1989, there was a resurgence of traditional country
music by artists like George Strait, Randy Travis, and Alan Jackson. The
industry exploded and continued to grow until 1994 and 1995.

I don't know how much the industry's success had to do with interest in
the South, cultural fads, southern presidents, and so on. If I could figure it
out, I'd be a genius. Some people attribute explosive success to the fact that
kids were gravitating toward and began to listen to Guns N' Roses, Nirvana,
and heavy rock and rap music, and radio responded; so other listeners, who
liked Bob Seger and the Eagles, the listeners who didn't like rap and heavy
rock, began to listen to country radio again. Many people in Nashville
believe that the big boom in country music occurred simply because consumers didn't have anyplace else to go that was comfortable for them.

The Setup

Bruce Hinton, a record guy, and Tony Brown, a creative guy, have run
MCA for a long time. Keith Stegall and I have the same kind of relationship. He does the creative stuff; I do the record stuff. We bounce off of each
other and it's sort of an ideal working relationship. There's a bit of a pat-
tern that's developing around the industry with setups like that. In the
past, most of the labels were run by producers. I think Joe Galante was the
first exception as a label head. Joe's way of doing things had a big influence on me. Joe is a great record guy.

Radio and Sales

Radio does not work hand in hand with the labels; but radio is prone to
follow our lead. Generally they'll play the single we release off of an album
as opposed to another song on the album.

In the music industry, sales is the whole game for us. Publishers and writers care about getting airplay (from which they receive royalties); but our bottom line's driven purely by how many records we sell; albeit without the airplay we wouldn't sell as many units. We don't make any money from ticket sales either. Cassettes are only about 30 percent of our sales because the quality of CDs is so much better. We ship our singles to radio stations on CDs.

The artists have to sell the songs. Some artists have had extensive touring experience and have a base audience, usually in a specific region. Toby Keith is a good example of this. He had been touring the Southwest for years before we signed him, and he had his own bus, his own band, and a fan base to work off of.

Audience response to the songs the artist sings live is not the criteria used to select singles because some songs go over better live, while other songs sell better on the radio. Also, a lot of new artists have never played before a big audience when we release their first album. So we select singles by using our ears and the ears of the people who work for the label. A hit song has a way of rearing its head pretty quickly when you play it for a lot of people who love music, so a consensus usually grows fairly strong as to what songs on that album are the hits.

Sometimes we have to second-guess and ask ourselves if radio might rather hear a love song or a cheating song. Radio hasn't been interested in playing many cheating songs lately. The big love ballads have gotten a lot of airplay—we call it prozac radio. They want everybody to feel good so they won't punch the button and go to another station.

The Writers

Keith Stegall has written dozens of hit songs, like "Don't Rock the Jukebox" for Alan Jackson and "Sexy Eyes" for Dr. Hook. Carson Chamberlain, who is also on staff, has written songs that have been recorded by Keith Whitley and Alan Jackson.

We don't just look to our writers for hit songs. There are a few people in our company whose job is to listen to songs submitted by publishers. Either they go to the publishing company and listen to the current songs by the writers at that company or they have a relationship with somebody who will bring them a song that they think is appropriate for a particular artist. Most labels will let all of the major publishers know when they're recording a new artist and try to get a tape to the publishers so that the publishers will know what the artist sounds like and what style of music they're going to be recording. After listening, the publishers pitch songs to the labels on the basis of what they've learned.

There used to be a lot of publishing splits, but now, if the publishing is split, it is usually because the song has several different writers. In the last several years in Nashville, cowriting seems to have increased. There are people writing with each other every day, all over town. If cowriting creates a hit song, then cowriting is a good way to write. Whenever we listen to songs, we try not to notice who wrote or published the song because sometimes we might be biased.

Some people in Nashville might tell you that in the old days the producer had part of the publishing, or the record company did, and I think that anybody who is trying to take publishing splits now is going to lose.

Labels should try to find the best songs they can find regardless of who wrote them or published them. If you're trying to play games, under the table, you're probably going to get your teeth kicked in.

Definitions

We asked one artist to cut his hair because his hairstyle resembled Billy Ray's, and we already had a Billy Ray. Then there's always the great hat debate. Terri Clark wears a hat and sometimes we question whether we should do some photo sessions without the hat.

If you were to speak to all of our artists, they would all tell you that we never made a decision about them that was against their will. I don't mean to sound self-righteous, just honest. It's hard enough to get out on stage when you're comfortable with yourself, let alone when someone has dressed you up and you don't feel comfortable. We use clothes, makeup, and hairstylists for our photo shoots and videos to supplement the efforts of our artists. We don't have any meetings around here saying that so-and-so needs to wear boots or whatever.

Although our artists are not on steady draws, some of them do receive cost-of-living expenses. We may help them pay their rent while they're making a record or are between album projects—I guess you could call this a draw or an advance. If we believe in our artists enough to make a record, we have to keep them fed while they're recording.

We also provide tour support for our artists. Before our artists have a hit big enough for them to get paid to play in front of audiences, we pick up most of their touring tab. Ideally, artists become self-sufficient and can play for around $3,000 to $5,000 a night. Out of that, they have to pay their band, their bus and driver, hotels, lights, sound, and so on. Their booking agent is supposed to talk a venue into paying them enough to cover their expenses and make a small profit, but if they can't then we pick up the tab. If there is any profit, then that profit is paid to the booking agent, the artist, and the artist's manager.

Changes

Some of my wishes may sound crazy because free enterprise rules, as it should; however, I wish there were more entrepreneurial opportunities for people who love music. Once there were people who began one small record store and were able to build their business into a chain of record stores. Once there were people who owned radio stations because they loved music and they programmed their stations for the pure enjoyment of music and not out of competition, greed, or politics. These were the people who loved music more than they loved money. I have a wish that, in the midst of consolidation of every major industry in America, the entrepreneurial opportunities are not squelched. I'd love to see someone be able to start an independent record label and thrive; start an independent record store and thrive; or own a radio station and thrive. I wish the enormous, consolidated, monolithic companies would become so inefficient that entrepreneurs could thrive once again.

It is very important to have faith that most of us who are in this business got into it because we love music. I certainly didn't think I would have a career and make a living in the music industry. I was just trying to make enough money to pay my rent so I could stay around the business. If you were to speak with most of the people who are in the music business, whether they're entertainers, executives, or whatever they do in the industry, I truly believe that their primary motivation for getting into the business would be because they loved music and their love for music overrode greed.

Goals

I had the dream of doing exactly what I'm doing. After my dream came true and I became reasonably successful at my job, I asked myself, "What's next?" I don't long to be an executive at a larger record company because I've worked for large companies like MCA in Los Angeles. I'm intrigued by the publishing end of the business, probably because it is as close to the creative process of writing and composing songs as you can get. I love the songs more than anything else about this business.

One of my heroes is Mo Ostin, who ran Warner Bros. Records for many years. Mo had a reputation for keeping the same employees and the same artist roster for years. He gave the artists and the employees a sense of security and longevity. There was a unity of purpose when Mo ran things. When I arrived in Nashville, I thought that, if I couldn't do anything else, I'd put together an artist roster and a group of employees who could all trust and enjoy each other's company and not feel insecure that I was going to leave or that they were going to be moved out.

Although it's nice to have new people join the company from time to time, there is a camaraderie among the people I work with that is of great importance to me. I'm enough of a jock that I like the team thing, and I'm enough of a family man that I like the family thing. At the moment, I must say that I am content. However, I do want to sell more records than Garth Brooks. His records sales, after all, are the benchmark to reach for.

Advice

You had better love music enough to be broke for a long time. You'll have to have an enormous amount of patience because it takes a long, long time to succeed in any aspect of this business. As in anything you ultimately achieve in this life, there is a history of dues paying, which equates to learning.

I began at the very bottom and worked my way up the ladder very slowly and managed to make enough money along the way to pay the rent and still be involved in music, as I said before. There certainly were moments when I could have left this business and made more money doing something else. There were also moments when there were down-turns in the industry that didn't allow for any growth, which in turn impeded opportunities.

When I've spoken with friends, children, nieces, and nephews who thought they wanted to get into this industry, I've told them that I'm not so sure—if I was looking at a career as opposed to just wanting to be around music, as the way to make a buck—that I would look at this indus-try. It's not in a growth state, and if you're looking for a career you need growth opportunities. The industry needs to grow in order for people to be promoted in a reasonable period of time. You have to be willing to work in a mail room or as a clerk in a record store, a gofer in a recording studio, a tape copy person in a publishing company. If you come out of college and think that it is time to buy that BMW, you better go to Wall Street and look for a job.

I was very fortunate to have gotten into the industry during one of its growth phases. I had the time to learn how to manage people by first manag-ing five, then ten, then twenty, then thirty. The learning curve was fine then, but I don't know whether I'd want to do it all over again, beginning now.

It's very sad that there are so many people who are out of work who are very proficient and have paid years of dues learning this industry. Recently, Rising Tide Records was shut down, and all of their employees are now out of work; some of those people had relocated to Nashville, all of them had worked at various companies perfecting what they did best, and now they're all out of work. Any newcomers who are trying to find positions in the industry are going to have to compete with all of the out-of-work experts looking for work.

There are some wonderful schools like Belmont University and Middle Tennessee State University that have excellent music business depart-ments. They can give a newcomer a leg up in terms of understanding the lingo, knowing their way around, networking, and receiving intern oppor-tunities, which many major labels offer. Interns work for as little as $50 a month and get free records and concert tickets while they continue to attend classes. What they learn from these opportunities is invaluable.

And the record labels are able to decide whether the interns have a good work ethic and the right kind of personality and where they might be well suited to be placed inside of a company. This is a wonderful way for a young person to enter the business.

However, I don't think it necessarily takes a formal education to succeed in the music industry; it takes a willingness to learn and a great love for music. I went to college for six years, but I never got my degree, so I don't think that a degree is critical. I've never asked anyone for their university credentials when they're applying at my company. However, I have asked them where they have worked and for how long. I don't remember having ever asked anyone what they may have studied in college.

Also, and I may be wrong, but I don't think it's who you know that gets you a job today. The best way to get to know someone is to go to work for them. So, if you can find a way to work in the music industry, even if you work for free, it is a great way to take that first step into the music industry.

Regardless of what you may want to do or be in the major music industry, it is important to remember that you will be competing with literally thousands of incredibly talented and gifted people, and the most gifted person doesn't always get the shot. Why? Bad timing and bad luck. You have got to have some luck.

I feel certain that there must be someone who is sitting out in the middle of the hinterlands who is gifted beyond belief, musically, and who hasn't figured out a way to find us. If you happen to be this person, then come to Nashville, wash some dishes, go to work singing your songs on a stool in a bar, connect with a publishing company and learn how to write (if you're inclined to write), and get yourself real ready before you walk into my office. Because although we're not necessarily looking for polish, we most definitely are looking for knowledge.

Lastly, I want to say that I've never had a morning come when I wasn't anxious to get up and go to work; and throughout my tenure in the music industry, I never felt as though I was particularly gifted; however, I most definitely feel as though I am blessed.

5

Mike Curb

Curb Records

Prosperity asks fidelity; adversity exacts it.

—Seneca

Mike Curb

Background

My father, Charles, was originally from Oklahoma City, Oklahoma. He graduated from the University of Oklahoma, went to law school, and later, during World War II, became an agent for the Federal Bureau of Investigation. The FBI stationed him in Savannah, Georgia, where I would be born on December 12, 1944.

My mother, Stella, who was an only child, grew up in Pittsburgh. She graduated from the University of Pittsburgh, then went to work on campus in one of the staff offices. My father was sent on a three-month assignment by the FBI to the campus where my mother worked. Eventually, they met, fell in love, and married.

A few years ago, my father passed away; however, my family sustains strength by staying in close touch with one another. Both my mother and my sister live in Los Angeles. My sister, Carole, has been with Curb Records since its inception. She is currently the president of our international branch, Curb Entertainment, which markets our products outside the United States. My mother, when both our schedules permit, visits me in Nashville, where I live with my wife, Linda, and my daughters, Courtney and Megan Carole.

After my parents were married, we lived in Savannah. We then moved to Charleston, South Carolina, where my sister was born. During those years, we moved quite a bit. From Charleston, we moved to Oklahoma City, Prescott, Arizona, and then to Compton, California. I began kindergarten when we arrived in Compton. Compton is not far from Watts. The area was going through a great transition at that time in terms of the diversity of races. When I went to school there, the student body was one-third Mexican-American, one-third African-American, and one-third Anglo-American. Growing up in this environment shaped and defined my outlook on society. I grew up color-blind, so to speak.

My grandparents also helped to formulate my early societal attitudes. My paternal grandfather, Charles Curb, was a Baptist minister from Oklahoma. My maternal grandfather, Charles Stout, was the director of the

YMCA in Pittsburgh. Both of my grandmothers were born in Texas. My paternal grandmother, Martha Kilgore Curb, was Irish-American. My maternal grandmother, Eloisa Salazar Stout, was of Mexican-American descent. Grandmother Stout was a strong and stoic woman. She was a very positive influence in my life.

When I was in the third grade, we moved to Van Nuys, California, and remained there until I was seventeen years old. During my high school years, I formed a musical group, which later became the Mike Curb Congregation. I played piano and guitar. My father provided well for the family, but we were not wealthy; therefore, if I wanted money for extras, such as my record collection, I was expected to earn it. I got a paper route when I was nine and continued on the same route until I was fourteen. I used some of my earnings to buy a guitar and an electric keyboard and periodically to add to my growing record collection.

My mother loved my music. When I would compose, she would tell me how wonderful my compositions were, even though I knew they weren't that good. When I played my piano, we'd sing together. When mother taught Sunday school, I'd play the church organ.

I was raised in a close-knit and loving family.

Early Recordings

My high school group, the Mike Curb Congregation, through word of mouth, networking, playing throughout the area, and having great reviews, caught the attention of some Word Record executives. Word was headquartered in Waco, Texas. I drove all the way to Waco from Los Angeles, to meet with and discuss our first recording with the label's executives. Eventually, we recorded about ten albums for Word Records.

The Sidewalk Leading to Curb

In 1964, when I was eighteen years old, I formed my corporation. Originally called Sidewalk Records, in 1969 the name would be changed to Curb Records. I had $3,000, which was payment for a song I had written entitled "You Meet the Nicest People on a Honda," which Honda used in one of their commercials. I used that money to set up my corporation. I didn't know much about the business of music at that time. I set up my corporation in order to have an outlet for my own recordings because no one else wanted to release them.

I learned by doing. Still in my teens, I was writing and composing songs, producing records, playing two instruments, singing, and negotiating recording deals for my company.

Signing Artists

It was in the late 1960s when I signed the Osmond family to my label. I produced or coproduced most of their hit records. Don Costa and I coproduced "Puppy Love," "Go Away Little Girl," and "They Try to Tell Us We're Too Young."

In 1974, when Donny and Marie emerged as a team, I had already merged my corporation with MGM, and I produced their albums *I'm Leavin' It All up to You* and *The Morning Side of the Mountain* for MGM/Curb. When Donny and Marie performed on their hit television show, I produced their album for the show, and I continued to produce all of their records throughout that three-year period. When Marie was thirteen years old, I produced her recording of "Paper Roses," which was a number 1 country record.

I signed Mel Tillis to MGM/Curb in the early 1970s. We had a number 1 country record titled "I Ain't Never." Mel went on to have a lot of hit records on MGM/Curb.

The Road to Success

In the latter part of 1969 or the early 1970s, our group crossed over into pop music. We were asked to record the music for the movie *Kelly's Heroes.* Clint Eastwood was the leading man, along with Telly Savalas. Lola Schiffren and I cowrote "Burning Bridges," the theme song for *Kelly's Heroes.* The song was a duet with Hank Williams Jr. and the Mike Curb Congregation. Since I was coproducer on the song, I flew to Nashville for the first time to get together with Hank in a Nashville recording studio. As it turned out, to our delight and amazement, that song became the very first number 1 song Hank ever had on the *Billboard* country charts.

On my return to California, I became the national president of MGM Records. I worked on the Culver City lot from 1969 until 1974, when Kirk Kerkorian, the majority stockholder and owner of MGM Records, sold the company to Polygram. When that sale occurred, I reestablished Curb Records.

During my years as president of MGM Records, I wrote some hit songs. I wrote Liza Minelli's theme song titled "It Was a Good Time." This was the song Liza sang to her mother, Judy Garland, as her closing song for her award-winning, live stage performance. I also wrote the album titled *Liza with a Z.* I also wrote and produced songs for Roy Orbison, Steve Lawrence and Eydie Gorme, Eddy Arnold, Andy Williams, and Donny and Marie Osmond. Other albums recorded by the Mike Curb Congregation included *Put Your Hand in The Hand* and *Softly Whispering I Love You.* We recorded a lot of music for Walt Disney, and we had a *Billboard* Top 10 single titled "It's a Small, Small World," which was the only hit recording of that song, from our hit album of the same name.

In 1971, one of the Mike Curb Congregation's most memorable recordings was our duet of "The Candy Man" with Sammy Davis Jr. That recording went to number 1 on the *Billboard* singles pop charts. This was our first number 1 pop record in *Billboard*. Our first number 1 country record in *Billboard*, was "All for the Love of Sunshine," the duet with Hank Williams Jr.

In 1972, I was named *Billboard's* number 1 producer of the year, which was my first major award. In 1975, I signed the Four Seasons. We were fortunate to have a Bob Guadio/Judy Parker song titled "Oh What a Night," which became a number 1 record. The Four Seasons began their second life when they signed with Curb Records. In 1976, thanks to Phil Gernhard, I signed the Bellamy Brothers. "Let Your Love Flow" was both a pop and a country hit. It went to number 1 on the *Billboard* country charts. I signed Shaun Cassidy, who had a big hit record with "Da Do Ron Ron" in 1977. Shaun was tremendously successful. He sold over ten million records in the late 1970s.

When I signed Debby Boone, we had the biggest single record MGM/Curb ever had, "You Light Up My Life." That was the number 1 record of the year in 1977. It was number 1 on the *Billboard* pop charts for ten weeks in a row, and it was also a country hit and a contemporary Christian hit, and Debby won the Grammy award for best new artist.

Curb Records was having many country hits even though our company was headquartered in California. During the 1970s, I made many trips to Nashville to record the country artists on our label. Many of our artists' records were receiving both pop and country acceptance: Donny and Marie Osmond, the Osmond Brothers, the Bellamy Brothers, Hank Williams Jr., Debby Boone, and Exile. We signed Exile in 1978. We recorded "Kiss You All Over," which also went to number 1 on the *Billboard* pop charts. Exile was a group from the South, and, although they had a huge pop hit, they went on to become country artists. In the late 1970s, we signed T. G. Sheppard, who had fifteen number 1 singles in *Billboard*, from the late 1970s through the 1980s.

When Hank Williams Jr. recovered from his horrible fall from a mountain, he once again signed with Curb Records and went on to have monumental success throughout the late 1970s and through the entire decade of the 1980s. His records were selling in the millions, which in Nashville in the 1970s, was unheard of. Back then, if an artist sold 100,000 records, they'd have a huge congratulatory party. In fact, Hank is still signed to Curb and is still doing very well. I wouldn't be surprised if he is one of the best-selling artists of all time. I believe that Hank Williams Jr. redefined country music by playing a progressive form of country music that was, at the same time, traditional.

108

Chapter 5

Politics

In the mid-1970s, I met Ronald Reagan at a Boys Club event where I was scheduled to speak. I appreciated what Reagan was trying to accomplish, and eventually I began to work for him during his campaign, although at the time I knew nothing about politics. If the polls were any indication, it looked like Reagan would win. Then Nixon resigned, and Gerald Ford was sworn in as president. When Ford became president, many people who had been working for Reagan left the campaign. However, I stayed on, and Reagan asked me to be his state chairman.

Two years after that, at Reagan's urging, I ran for lieutenant governor of California. I was elected even though the seated governor was Jerry Brown, a Democrat. From 1979 to 1982, I served as lieutenant governor of California. This was the first time that California ever had a governor and lieutenant governor from different parties. In 1980, Governor Jerry Brown ran for the presidency and he left California to campaign for about one year. So, I became acting governor of California in Brown's absence. I still owned Curb Records, although I was not actively participating in the company business. Dick Whitehouse became president of Curb Records. He did a great job during my absence. He made frequent trips to Nashville and signed many fine artists to our label.

Back to Music

I actively returned to Curb in 1983. That was the year we signed the Judds. In 1984 we signed Sawyer Brown, and in 1985 Lyle Lovett. Lyle began as a country artist with records like "Cowboy Man" prior to becoming a pop artist. In 1986 we signed the Desert Rose Band. Most of the artists we signed were more country than pop, like Hal Ketchum, who we signed in the early 1990s.

Moving to Nashville

In the 1970s, we were having country hits with Marie Osmond, the Bellamy Brothers, T. G. Sheppard, Debby Boone, Mel Tillis, and the Osmond Brothers. In the late 1980s, we bought a building and opened an office in Nashville. But this was primarily an office used to promote our artists and not an office to run the business. Our business was still being run out of Burbank, California. The office building we owned in Burbank was in the thick of things, right near Warner Bros., Universal Studios, and Disney Studios.

In the mid- to late 1980s and early 1990s, we were having great success with Lyle Lovett, Hank Williams Jr., Sawyer Brown, the Judds, and the

Desert Rose Band, but we still had our offices in California. We always worked with other companies. Co-ventures included the Judds on Curb/RCA, Hank Williams Jr. on Curb/Warner, Sawyer Brown on Curb/Capitol, and Lyle Lovett on Curb/MCA. These co-ventures made us realize that if we ever wanted to properly market our artists-to-be on our own label with our own marketing department and our own promotional department, and not form co-ventures with other labels, we would have to move to Nashville. I never defined or categorized our music, and we had a lot of pop hits along with our country hits. But throughout the 1970s and 1980s, we were definitely becoming more and more country oriented.

Finally, with Hal Ketchum's 1992 success with "Small Town Saturday Night," and "Past the Point of Rescue," we moved to Nashville. Now, in the 1990s, we own, run, and solely operate our companies, and Curb Records is the only label that's a Tennessee corporation. Most of the other labels are owned by multinational corporations.

Success

In 1991, during our transitional period, the number 1 single of the year for *R&R* [*Radio & Records*] was "Small Town Saturday Night," recorded by Hal Ketchum. Hal impacted the music industry in 1992 with his gold album *Past the Point of Rescue*. Along with the successes of Hal Ketchum, in 1992 Wynonna Judd became a solo artist and garnered *Billboard's* number 1 single record of the year with her recording of "I Saw the Light." Wynonna also had *Billboard's* number 1 album of the year, *Wynonna*. She became the first female artist to sell five million albums on her first solo album release. That number of album sales was never duplicated by a female artist until 1997, when our company released *Blue* on LeAnn Rimes.

Lyle Lovett was making a transition into being a multimarket artist. Lyle's music expressed all genres: alternative, pop, jazz, blues, and rock. But Lyle has a lot of country in his soul. Sawyer Brown was also making their major transition to country with their big hit "Some Girls Do" and "Thank God For You" in 1993. In 1994, Tim McGraw broke into stardom. Tim won *Billboard's* album of the year award for *Not a Moment Too Soon*. He also had recorded the hit singles "Indian Outlaw" and "Don't Take the Girl." Later that same year, Tim coproduced Jo Dee Messina on Curb Records. Jo Dee had a hit single in 1996 with "Heads Carolina, Tails California."

Sometimes I Have to Pinch Myself

In 1997, *Billboard* named Curb Records the number 1 country album and the number 1 country singles label of the year. Winning both of these prestigious awards was a first for an independently owned record label.

In the December 1997 issue of *Time* magazine, there was an article titled "Can Garth Save Country?" The third paragraph of the article stated that I was doing too well in Nashville to worry about it: "Mike Curb, a Californian [. . .] in another life, produced hits by the Four Seasons, the Osmond family, and Debby Boone." I found it interesting that the writer of the article used the term "in another life" to refer to my career credits and awards in California. It is like another life because I hadn't won a *Billboard* award since 1972, when I was *Billboard*'s record producer of the year.

Even stranger than winning *Billboard* awards twenty-five years apart was the fact that, in 1997, LeAnn Rimes achieved success with Curb Records like Debby Boone had achieved with Curb Records in 1977, with the same song and album title, *You Light up My Life.* I coproduced *You Light up My Life* with LeAnn's father, Wilbur, and Chuck Howard. LeAnn's album was the first album in the history of music to debut at number 1 on the *Billboard* pop charts, number 1 on the *Billboard* country charts, and number 1 on the *Billboard* contemporary Christian charts. LeAnn won the Grammy award for best new artist exactly twenty years after Debby Boone had won the same award for her phenomenal success—with the same song!

Sometimes I have to pinch myself to make sure I am not dreaming, especially when I read articles indicating that Curb Records is the number 1 country music company in America. I did not move my family to Nashville strictly because of the music industry. My wife and I wanted our daughters to be raised in the South. We did not move to Nashville with the idea of being number 1, but one of our goals was to become a Tennessee corporation and to market our own records and be in control of our own destiny.

Departments and Divisions

Our video department won the *Billboard* award for the number 1 video with Ray Stevens. Our video department is run by Sue Austin. We market commercial videos like the Ray Stevens video. Sue also oversees and produces the videos we make on our artists, which are used for promotional purposes on CMT, TNN, and VH1.

I oversee our A&R department. Our A&R director is Michelle Metzger; publicity is headed by Liz Cavanaugh; finance is headed by Michael Huddleston; international is headed by my sister, Carole Curb Nemoy; business affairs and legal is headed by Tracy Moore; Tanya Dureaux heads up our copyright department; marketing is headed by Brad Holiday; publishing is headed by Meredith DeVoursney; sales is run by Bensen Curb; and our general manager is Dennis Hannon.

We have four operative label divisions. Curb/Christian, our contemporary division, is run by Clair Parr; promotion for our pop label is run by

Ric Lippincott. We have three country label divisions: Curb/Nashville, headed by Eva Wood and John Brown; Curb/MCG (Mike Curb Group) promotional unit, headed by Jeff Hackett; and Curb/Universal, headed by Gerrie McDowell and my cousin, John Curb.

Becky Judd is my personal assistant. I have an excellent staff of people working for Curb. As you read, you'll find that there are many females at the label. I believe that women make great executives; they are a tremendous asset to our company.

LeAnn Rimes

In 1995, my wife Linda, myself, and my daughters, Megan Carole and Courtney, were driving to the Smoky Mountains for a little vacation. That Friday, Linda came to my office to pick me up for our trip. I got into our car carrying my little brown briefcase, which is always filled with thirty to sixty tapes. These tapes are submitted to our company during the week by those seeking to be signed to a label as an artist or writer. Some of the tapes contain material to be listened to for our existing artists, but primarily these are tapes that are sent to people who work in our offices. Sometimes I'll receive tapes from friends, successful producers, and even unknown people who have brought their tape to the front desk of our offices.

As we were getting ready to drive away, Benson came to me and said, "There's a tape I haven't had the time to listen to. It's a tape of a teenage girl. I got the tape from a person I work with in the distribution department in Dallas, Texas. He heard the girl sing the National Anthem at a Dallas Cowboys football game and thought I should listen to it. But I haven't had the time, so would you mind taking it along and listening on your way up to the mountains?" I put the tape in my case along with forty or so other tapes, and we set out on our three-to-four-hour drive to the mountains.

First we listened to a new album by the Fun Factory, who are already signed to Curb. The Fun Factory is composed of two white artists and two black artists. They had a big hit song with "I Wanna Be with You." It received a lot of airplay. It was a very hypnotic song, and my daughters loved it.

Then one of my daughters said, "Dad, we've listened to the music you've wanted to listen to for an hour. Now we want to listen to the radio for a while." So we turned on the radio and listened to some alternative music. Then, about an hour later, as it was getting dark and I could no longer read the labels on the tapes, I pulled out another tape and popped it into the tape deck.

It turned out to be LeAnn Rimes singing "Blue." I played it for a few more minutes and said, "This can't be right. This doesn't sound like a thirteen-year-old girl." I took the tape out of the player to study it and finally said, "What a voice. She is really different." My oldest daughter said, "Dad, she is really a very special singer. She's great."

We were all very impressed with the tape. I played the entire tape twice. There were ten songs on the tape. Some were Christian songs, and some were country standards like "Country Sweetheart." I believe that was the tape she was making available at her concerts for her fans. In any event, we liked it.

We had our minivacation and were returning to Nashville on Sunday when my youngest daughter said, "Dad, maybe we should listen to the LeAnn Rimes tape again." So we did, and by the time we were halfway home we stopped for gas and called the number on the tape, which belonged to her attorney and manager, Lyle Walker, from Dallas. After we talked to Lyle, he called LeAnn's father, Wilbur, and we told him how much we liked the tape. The Rimes family drove to Nashville early the following day and arrived in Tennessee in time for dinner that Monday night.

That night Kyle Walker, LeAnn, Wilbur, and LeAnn's mother (Belinda), along with my family, all stood in line at the Cracker Barrel restaurant. The Cracker Barrel doesn't take reservations, but the food is good and the girls wanted to eat there. We certainly didn't feel very important standing in line for forty-five minutes.

About an hour into our dinner, my oldest daughter, Megan Carole, who was becoming bored with all the business talk and who is very direct in her views, suggested that she, Courtney and LeAnn either go to a movie or go out to look at their horses. Courtney was thirteen at the time, and Megan Carole was sixteen and had just begun to drive. I always worry when my daughters are out together. So, you can't imagine how worried I was when my girls and LeAnn drove off in the car, after dark, going either to see horses or to a movie. But, LeAnn later said in an article written about her, "One of the reasons I signed with Curb Records is because I liked Mike Curb's daughters, Courtney and Megan Carole." My daughters often remind me of LeAnn's article.

I wanted to sign LeAnn because there hadn't been a teenage artist for twenty-five years and because LeAnn has an awesome talent. The last teenage artist who had a hit was Marie Osmond in 1972. Tanya Tucker hit with "Delta Dawn" in 1968 or 1969, and Brenda Lee hit in the 1950s. I had signed Marie Osmond when she was thirteen years old and she had a big country hit with "Paper Roses." That was the last time a teenage girl had a hit, and I knew the odds against a teenager making it big were tremendous. I also wanted to sign LeAnn because I thought it would be a good opportunity for my daughters to see how the business works and to be part of the process. It's not an easy process getting the artist ready for videos, getting the album right, getting the mixes in the studio right, and getting the tracks mastered correctly.

When Wilber Rimes and I coproduce records, although Wilbur had never produced a record before, he intuitively understood how a record is supposed to feel. The feel of a record is the most important aspect, and that's exactly the way I produce records; so we work extremely well together. I have never had a great deal of technical training, so I go for the feel, that is, the emotions, the sound that the record is imparting to the emotional side of me. If a record feels good, hopefully the listener will want to play it over and over again. Wilbur was never affected by Nashville's rules. When a record felt good to him it was time to release it. We have also identified with each other because Wilbur, like me, never gives up. He made forty mixes of "Blue." Everything had to feel right—the mikes, the echo effects, and so on. Many major producers wouldn't understand what Wilbur and I are trying to achieve in the studio. Each one of LeAnn's records has a distinctly different sound. They are not like most of the records coming out of Nashville in the 1990s.

You don't have to have had fifty hits. You don't have to be technically skilled to make a great record. You do have to have that intangible ability to feel the sound, the emotions; after all, the sound, and the emotions evoked by that sound, is what creativity is all about.

After the musical process is completed, our company starts the whole process of marketing, promoting, and publicizing the record. In LeAnn's case, everything worked perfectly. In eighteen months, she had accomplished more than any other artist in that period of time. According to *Billboard* magazine in 1997, LeAnn Rimes is the number 1 pop artist, pop album artist, country artist, and country female artist and had the number 1 country singles sales for "How Do I Live" and the number 1 country album. In fact, "How Do I Live," which I coproduced with Wilbur and Chuck Howard, became the biggest-selling country single of all time, with sales in excess of three million records.

By the end of 1997, Curb Records had become *Billboard's* number 1 country label for both albums and singles. SoundScan confirmed that Curb Records had become the number 1 country record company in the United States.

If I Could Change Things

The music industry, like any other billion-dollar multifaceted industry, has many ups and downs. One of the biggest problems in our industry is when some record label executives don't stay with the artist long enough during their development stage and after the record is released. Some companies give up too soon. For example, I stuck with LeAnn and her album *Blue*. Tim McGraw was on his sixth single release when he broke with "Indian Outlaw." There were believers and nonbelievers. "Good Night

Sweetheart" took twenty-five weeks to develop, but once it came out it really put David Kersh over the top.

Goals

My short-term goals are the same as my long-term goals. I want to continue developing new artists and take my current artists to the next level in their careers.

Properly developing artists from the first stage to the top is extremely important in the creative process. It is also critical to continually reevaluate professional standards and to correct any weaknesses which may be found in your company. Also, it is necessary to keep the standards of creative excellence very high among all of the people in all of the different departments.

If You Want to Succeed

If you want to be successful, pick an area or a direction that you totally believe in, whether you're an artist, a publisher, an accountant, a background singer, or a session musician—whatever it is that you excel at, concentrate on that area and become the best you can be. Anyone who is an expert in any one area of the business, in my opinion, will be successful. However, if you try to be an expert in too many areas, I think you will be sacrificing your greatest talent because you are not giving that talent all of your attention.

I draw on the expertise of other executives who are more skilled than I may be in certain areas. My particular expertise lies in the creative processes. I understand that end of the business—how records are developed from the perspective of a producer. I combine my areas of expertise with my marketing, sales, and promotion people's expertise. We work together by combining all areas of knowledge to create a successful product.

I listen to people who work for me. If the head of my promotional department hears that a song on an album is getting attention in a particular market, then I will listen to that song again and reconsider my previous viewpoints given new information. Marketing people pick up sales activity in a particular region. This new information may also alter my first impression of a record. So I go back and listen to that record again with a different point of view.

We have a close working relationship at my company. We all work together to achieve the highest degree of success possible in all creative areas.

6

Joe Galante

RCA Label Group—RLG
(RCA and BNA Records)

Courtesy of Peter Nash

What we have to learn to do, we learn by doing.

—Aristotle

About the RCA Label Group (RLG)

The RCA Label Group (RLG), which consists of RCA and BNA Records, is likely the best-known record label group operating out of Nashville. It's certainly the one with the longest history and the most familiar logo.

The first country recording ever made is, in fact, the property of RCA. Eck Robertson and Henry Gilliland walked into the New York offices of the Victor Talking Machine Company on June 30, 1922, one of them wearing a Confederate soldier uniform, the other dressed as a cowboy. They talked the label executives into letting them record a couple of fiddle tunes, "Sally Goodin'" and "Arkansas Traveler," setting the stage for an industry that now nets a reported $2 billion annually. Victor was more committed to country music than any other record company during the Roaring Twenties, with Ralph Peer making numerous talent-scouring trips throughout the southeast. On one of those trips, he recorded Jimmie Rodgers and the Carter Family in Bristol.

In 1929, the Radio Corporation of America, which had founded its own record label in October 1919, purchased Victor, and the company was known as RCA Victor for years to come. RCA would build upon the Rodgers/Carter legend by adding stars such as Eddy Arnold and Hank Snow—both future members of the Country Music Hall of Fame, as were the Carters and Rodgers, proving its mettle with both traditional country sounds and smoother pop-oriented material.

The same year that RCA took over the Victor assets, a New Jersey high school student, Steve Sholes, took on a part-time job with the label. Steve Sholes would remain with the company his entire life, becoming the A&R head for both country and R&B recordings in 1945. Sholes was responsible for signing both Arnold and Snow as well as Jim Reeves, Pee Wee King, and a guitarist named Chet Atkins, whom he envisioned as a rival to the already-established Merle Travis.

Atkins proved to be a widely talented figure. His stellar guitar work made him a regular sideman on Nashville sessions and the Grand Ole Opry, but he quickly emerged as a musician with enviable taste as well. Sholes continued to base his operations out of New York, and on the occasions when he was unable to make the trek to Nashville for recording sessions, he left the proceedings under Atkins's direction. By 1957, Atkins was in control of the company's entire country operation.

Among Atkins' first moves was to convince the label it could benefit from owning its own recording studio in Nashville. Thus, at a cost of $39,515, RCA Studio B was opened in 1957 at the corner of 17th Avenue and Hawkins Street, today known as Roy Acuff Place. The studio stood for some twenty years, providing a recording site for such projects as Hank Snow's "I've Been Everywhere," Dottie West's "Here Comes My Baby," the Everly Brothers's "Cathy's Clown," Elvis Presley's "Are You Lonesome Tonight," and Floyd Cramer's "Last Date." The studio is now an annex of the Country Music Hall of Fame.

Atkins took over RCA at a time when the country genre was under fire, thanks in large part to one of Sholes's more astute signings. Sholes signed Elvis Presley to RCA in a legendary November 1955 deal that saw the so-called Hillbilly Cat's contract purchased for a then-record $35,000. Presley led the charge of rock 'n roll, which inspired teenage spending on music in a manner previously unrivaled. In addition, Presley became the top-selling recording artist in history, certainly the top seller for RCA, which, in its lengthy history, has represented such acts as Enrico Caruso, the Guess Who, Perry Como, John Denver, Hall and Oates, and the Dave Matthews Band.

As a result of Presley's sales surge in the late 1950s, sales for country music dropped dramatically, and Nashville quickly grew concerned about the future of its primary music form. Along with Decca head Owen Bradley, Atkins made some major alterations in country music, downplaying the role of fiddle and the steel guitar and replacing them with small string sections and pop-flavored background vocal groups, such as the Jordanaires and the Anita Kerr Singers. The resulting cosmopolitan texture was dubbed "the Nashville sound," illustrated by such Atkins-produced classics as Jim Reeves's "He'll Have to Go," Eddy Arnold's "Make the World Go Away," and Skeeter Davis's "The End of the World." While the Nashville sound would later come under fire from some country music purists who believed that Atkins and Bradley had "sold out," their redefinition of the genre brought country to a larger popularity than it had ever enjoyed.

Under Atkins, RCA continued to evolve, with the signings of such acts as Waylon Jennings, Charley Pride, Bobby Bare, and Dolly Parton. Both Jennings and Parton would figure prominently in the label's future, even after Atkins had stepped aside in favor of Jerry Bradley, the son of Owen.

During Bradley's reign, both Parton and Ronnie Milsap rose to prominence as pop-oriented country superstars, while Jennings was part of a
revolutionary album *Wanted: The Outlaws*, which became the first country
album officially recognized for selling more than 1 million copies. Featuring music from Jennings, Jessi Colter, Willie Nelson, and Tompall Glaser,
the *Outlaws* became the centerpiece in the late 1970s "outlaw" movement,
which represented a move away from the slick productions of the Nashville sound, and toward a more raw approach that often melded country
music with basic, tough rock attitudes.

Near the end of the Bradley era, the label signed Alabama, a southern
rock-bred hybrid that returned the band concept to a major role in country music. For years, labels had resisted group acts, fearing that the public
would be unable to identify with the band and that if it achieved any success,
it would break up, dashing the label's economic investment. Instead,
Alabama proved wildly successful, setting a record with twenty-one consecutive number 1 singles. Along the way, their energetic shows attracted
a youthful audience, further expanding the reach of country music.

Much of their surge came under Joe Galante, a former New Yorker who
had been transferred to Nashville and learned the country way from
Bradley and Atkins. Determined and confident, Galante came from a mar-
keting/finance background and was one of the first to use extensive market research in setting the policies for a record label. Alabama, Clint Black,
the Judds, Keith Whitley, Lorrie Morgan, and Earl Thomas Conley all
became major contributors to the label, and in 1990 Galante was rewarded
by being tapped to head RCA's entire pop division in New York, where
the label's American operations are based.

Four years later, however, he requested a return to Nashville, where he
continues to run RCA and its sister label, BNA, established in 1991. Taking its initialed name from Nashville's airport, Berryfield Nashville Airport, BNA set the tone for a 1990s development in which many of Nashville's labels split in an attempt to widen their market share. But, as the
trend created an overabundance of record companies, most of those labels
failed to show a profit, and BNA also began the trend of being absorbed
into the parent company or simply being eliminated. Today, RCA and
BNA collectively represent such acts as Alabama, Clint Black, Lorrie Morgan, Lonestar, Mindy McCready, and Restless Heart.

RCA has made great use of its trademark mascot, Nipper, a dog
entranced by a gramophone in a classic painting titled *His Master's Voice*.
Born in 1884, Nipper was adopted by English painter Francis Barraud,
who noted the Jack Russell terrier's fascination with Thomas Edison's talking machine. The dog died in 1895 and was buried under a mulberry tree
in London, but five years later his likeness was registered with the U.S.
Patent Office, and the painting was later sold to an English businessman.

When a Victor executive spotted the painting in the businessman's office, he engineered a deal to make Nipper the trademark for Victor and, after the company's 1929 sale, RCA.

That trademark has returned, in a manner of speaking, to the continent where the real Nipper lived his life. RCA was purchased from then-owner General Electric in September 1986 by BMG, a West German entertainment firm. BMG distributes not only RCA and BNA Records but also the product of Arista Records, whose country label handles such acts as Brooks & Dunn, Alan Jackson, Pam Tillis, and Diamond Rio.

Joe Galante

New York

I was born on December 18, 1949, in Queens, New York. My father was a postman. My mother was a secretary. Marianne and Ann are my two younger sisters. Other than listening to and appreciating good music, my immediate family had no ties to the music industry, and my interest in the music business evolved after graduating from college.

As a teen, the Beatles and the Rolling Stones were two of my favorite groups. Around that time, some of my high school friends formed a small band, and electric rhythm guitar was my instrument of choice. After graduating from high school, the next four years were spent getting degrees in marketing and finance from Fordham University.

During my senior year, the university coordinated a career day with several companies. Representatives from General Electric, the Federal Reserve Bank of New York, and RCA came and spoke to the senior students regarding the possibility of careers with their respective companies. Various representatives of different companies interviewed me at that time, and RCA made me an offer. Although General Electric made me an offer, I couldn't get excited about it because they were involved with nuclear power projects. And the Federal Reserve Bank was not creative enough to excite me.

RCA/New York

In 1970, when I interviewed, Rocco Lagginesttra was RCA's president. At that time, I believe they had five different companies under the RCA umbrella. I interviewed with Coronet Carpets, Banquet Foods, NBC, and RCA's respective television division. RCA had recently integrated a computer division as a part of the conglomerate companies, and, although I was interested, the interviewer felt that in order to understand all of the intricacies of computers I would have had to have either a masters degree or a doctorate.

During my interview with the record division I was offered a job in their finance department. I promptly replied, "I don't want to work in a record

120

company. I don't want to keep records." I thought he was talking about financial records and keeping them filed and organized. I didn't even know that RCA was a record company because I didn't have any RCA records in my collection.

When I realized that the interviewer was talking about working in the finance department of the record label, I was interested, and he made arrangements for me to go see the people at the label division. Once there, I was asking, "Who do you have on the label?" I was told about many guys who were about to happen; however, they never happened. The only artists I had heard of who were on RCA were Perry Como and Elvis Presley. However, I was only twenty years old at that time, and Como was hardly an icon to me.

So I thought to myself that I wasn't all that excited about the music being made at the label. I was cocky enough to think to myself, "Man, you guys are the most uncool label in the world." But, since they offered me $500 more a year than any of my other offers, I took the job. Also, I thought that in a few years I would be moved out of the finance department to one of their other divisions. My decision to go to work for RCA was strictly a pragmatic decision and had nothing to do with being interested in the music the label was making.

I was the administrator for financial analysis. Basically, I analyzed costs and made recommendations to the various departments, that is, the purchasing and promotion departments, which extended into my job description. Although I was just a peon working for others who were in management positions, I analyzed all of the areas and all costs involved in their areas within the departments, and then made suggestions as to how they might control some of their expenses. Actually, I learned a great deal. Although I didn't realize it at the time, the knowledge I gained was extremely beneficial to me later on. After all, in order to make a company successful and profitable, you have to know all of the ins and outs of running the company.

During the year and a half I held this position, and as I became more familiar with the various departments within the label, I began to have a particular affinity and interest in the promotion department. At that time, Frank Mancini was the vice president of the promotion department. Frank spent a lot of time teaching me the ropes. He invited me out to dinner with the promotion staff, which I thought was pretty smart of him because the closer he became with the guy analyzing various departmental costs, the more lenient I might become toward his department.

Aside from the fact that Frank was a terrific guy, I fell in love with the business. I was interested in taking the product to radio stations and building relationships with the people who play the music. For the next nine months, I continued to learn all I could from my friendship with Frank and the rest of the promotion staff when a position became available in that department. So I left the finance department and moved over to promotion. I worked in promotion for a short time and became very interested in product management.

As a result of my enthusiasm and hard work, I was moved into product management [today called A&R]. The company allowed to me to take on some of the artists signed to the label who weren't doing very well. I found myself working with David Bowie, Lou Reed, and several other phenomenal people. At the time, RCA hadn't realized the potential of these artists. Other than making sure that the guys showed up on time to play at various venues, there really wasn't much to manage; the talent was in place, as was their know-how as to how to present their talents.

I did, however, absorb a great deal of knowledge by being out on the road with these acts. I learned how to coordinate and initiate their meeting and greeting various people at their performances who could benefit their careers. I selected the press photos that I believed would be of the greatest commercial value in introducing them to the media and the public. I learned the basics of how to deal with the customers who would be buying, servicing, and promoting the product. I worked in this capacity for about one year as well as continuing to work with the finance department.

Nashville: Culture Shock

Mel Ilberman, who currently works as senior executive vice president at Sony Records, was in charge of business affairs at RCA. One day, Mel called me into his office at RCA and asked me if I would mind going to Nashville, Tennessee. He said, "We have a program we would like to set you up on, to go down there for about two years and learn what you can and help them in any way they indicate they may need your help. The Nashville company is struggling right now." I said, "No. I have no interest in country music." About two weeks later, Mel again said, "I think you should go to Nashville and get to know the guys running our country division."

Having no choice, in 1973 I moved to Nashville. I met Chet Atkins, who was the president of RCA/Nashville, and Jerry Bradley [Owen Bradley's son], who was Chet's right hand. Although he was head of the company, Chet was also the creative guru. Jerry was in charge of the hard business aspects. Having sales of only $5 million and only forty acts on their roster, RCA/Nashville was hardly a viable business at that time.

Jerry took me to lunch and introduced me to various people; however, Jerry wasn't what one would call warm and fuzzy. He wasn't too thrilled to have a New York guy down here in his business, and I wasn't too thrilled to be in Nashville. I went back to New York and said, "Well, he really doesn't want me there, and I don't want to be there." I talked with my wife, Regina, about moving to Nashville. We were both resistant to the idea. We had a new baby daughter, Lynette, and were well settled in our lives. After discussing everything with my family, I told Mel, "I'm not moving to Nashville." But Mel said, "You're going to go to Nashville."

I was very unhappy about this country music situation. Having grown up in New York, I knew very little about it. I had heard of and listened to Johnny Cash because Cash wasn't totally country. But that was about the extent of my desire to learn anything about that genre of music. When I listened to Hank Snow and Porter Wagoner, I thought, "Oh, no. This is definitely not my kind of music."

Also, New York was very exciting for me. I was meeting talented, energetic people who were moving ahead in a fast-paced and vibrant social context. I was meeting people like Thomas Mottola, who was working for John Oates and Daryl Hall and is now CEO for Sony Music, and Randy Hoffman, who recently managed Mariah Carey. I was meeting so many incredible people who would go on to run major companies. I thought, "Who in the world am I going to meet in Nashville, and why am I going?" In Nashville in 1973, there was hardly a downtown area, few restaurants, a tiny airport, and next to no nightlife—it was total culture shock for me. To add to all these negatives, the people who ran the music business kept a closed shop. If you weren't from Nashville, you were not wanted.

In April 1973, I bought a home in Brentwood, an upscale residential neighborhood about twenty minutes from the heart of Nashville's tiny business area. The Brentwood area was very isolated in 1973. Regina and I were used to having many friends close by, and we missed New York a great deal. We were not too thrilled with our current lack of social contacts. —I was placed in the administrative area of the company, and I was supposed to figure out how to make the company grow. RCA had only about forty acts, and thirty of those forty acts were singles acts who were totally obscure, and no one knew their names. So, I struggled along, trying not to get in anyone's way and trying do my job—which loosely construed, was working with Jerry Bradley—the best way I could under strained circumstances. I continued in this capacity for about one year. I totally respected Bradley's concerns about my being there. We were from two different worlds, and neither one of us knew exactly what I was supposed to be doing. New York did not specifically define my job criteria. I was just more or less told to go to Nashville and work with Bradley.

Transitions

All of the Nashville operations were A&R centers. Departmental transactions regarding sales, promotion, publicity, and artwork were still reported to the New York office. Nothing originated in Nashville, with the exception of actually making the records. Eventually, Jerry and I went to New York to attend an administrative meeting regarding RCA/Nashville. During the meeting, I spoke up on behalf of the Nashville label. I explained to the New York executives that the guys in Nashville understood that market better than they did, so why not give them the responsibility to market the Nashville product?

After Jerry and I attended a few more New York meetings, Jerry realized that I was fighting the guys in New York on his behalf and on behalf of RCA/Nashville. Therefore, our relationship began to warm considerably. Jerry never did anything wrong toward me—he just didn't know why I was there. Before Jerry warmed to me, the only help accorded me was from a man named Frank Mancini, who came to Nashville to work on the marketing for crossover product, that is, country/pop. Frank introduced me to Buddy Lee of Buddy Lee Attractions and some other key people who Frank was familiar with.

Frances Preston, who at that time was the only woman in the entire Nashville music business who was in a position of power, was in charge of the BMI/Nashville office and helped me out by introducing me to people she knew and explaining the Nashville way of doing things to me. Frances helped me a great deal by speaking highly about me to the people she knew and worked with, and to this day Frances and I are still very good friends.

Nashville is a town that runs, to a large extent, on innuendo and rumor. There were ridiculous rumors that I was a Yankee spy. When I heard that, I thought, "What? Spy for what? Who am I supposed to be spying on?" I was typical New York, where you sometimes speak first and think later. My response to those rumors was, "There is no one here that I am interested in enough to spy on. Some of you people have overly inflated egos." Sometimes people are very quick to put newcomers in the grave if the newcomers don't have a few well-placed friends. People in the South are far more sensitive about words than are people in New York. It took some time for me to understand and appreciate the southern way of doing things.

Jerry was a producer and offered to teach me all the ins and outs of producing acts in the Nashville studios. He also was a believer, as I am, in understanding the history behind the ventures we worked on. As I continued to learn from Jerry, I took on added responsibilities. I would study the country singles charts in the various trade magazines. As I analyzed the songs on the charts I would approach Jerry and say, "This record is moving on up the charts for a competitive label, so perhaps it would help if we would do more promotion work on various records on RCA in order to push them on up the charts." Jerry considered my suggestions and would let the promotion department know how he intended to change certain promotion tactics.

This went on, successfully for some time, until Jerry said, "Guess what? You now have the full responsibility of analyzing the charts." I said, "I don't know anything about the charts on *Billboard, Gavin, Record World,* and *R&R (Radio & Record)*." He responded, "You've been moanin' and groanin' so much about how we should promote our records, why don't you take the reins and show me what you can do." This situation proved rather difficult for me because, although I had chart responsibility, I had no responsibility for the promotion staff. So I began to get to know national promotion guys who worked with our promotion staff. I dug in and started to learn all I could about promoting and marketing records.

The Turning Point: 1974 to 1976

What really turned me around, regarding my New York music genre attitude, was meeting and befriending Dolly Parton, Waylon Jennings, and Ronnie Milsap. I fell in love with them and their music. For a guy who grew up on the Beatles, the Rolling Stones, and Cream, I thought, "Man, this is it. I have found something that I can really sink my teeth into."

Dolly Parton

Dolly was still working on television with Porter Wagoner, and during commercial breaks she would pull those awful towels out of boxes of detergent. Dolly and I became very good friends, and we had a great deal of mutual respect for each other. We began working hard on her career.

There was a place in New York called the Felt Forum, now the Paramount Theater. The Forum was located just below Madison Square Garden. This was the venue where country acts would regularly perform their token shows in New York. They performed token shows because the best we could do was to have a couple of thousand seats filled, so the artist would only do one show per gig.

Our show included Bobby Bare and Charley Pride, and Dolly was supposed to open the show. Dolly decided to ride the Long Island Railroad from Jamaica Queens all the way to the end of the south shoreline and back. At each stop, she would get on a flatbed truck, all by herself, and sing "Love Is Like a Butterfly" acoustically. This was how she was advertising our show. It was decided that since I was from New York, I should accompany Dolly on her trek. So Dolly, myself, and Dolly's friend Judy Ogle went on the railroad from 7 A.M. to 4 P.M. We did this all day long. Dolly had incredible energy. Having spent so many hours with her we really got to know each other. Dolly is a great person with a wonderful sense of humor. We had a ball doing those railroad runs—a memory I'll always cherish.

In 1987, Dolly's option with RCA had come up, and she decided to leave the label. Dolly and I were riding in the back of a limo coming back from having had dinner when she said, "I know you love me, and I know everybody in Nashville loves me, but I don't think that the rest of the company understands what they have to do to move my career along." Looking back, I know she was absolutely correct, but at the time I felt as though one of my kids was about to leave home. She went on to sign with Columbia Records, but nothing eclipsed the success she had had with RCA. But she was correct about getting more attention at another company because no one at RCA was interested in making pop records on Dolly at that time. Currently, she is on Decca Records. Whether or not she was right or wrong in leaving RCA I cannot say; history will have to make that judgment.

Ronnie Milsap

In the early and mid-1970s, Ronnie was doing shows in a lot of different clubs around the country. He was still playing in Roger Miller's King of the Road Club at the top of the hotel in a little circular ballroom club. He used to play both country and the old Motown sound. Ronnie, although not a songwriter like Dolly, had a wonderful voice. He was a fine talent and a wonderful entertainer. Being blind, he both educated me and caused me to have a lot of appreciation for all he overcame so effortlessly. At times, Ronnie, who weighed 210 pounds and was six-foot-three, would ask me to guide him around. I learned real quick when to stop and when to start walking again so as not to get in his way, since he was about twice my size.

It was a joint decision when Ronnie left RCA. He left the label about the same time that Dolly left. You reach a point where an artist has had a fifteen- or twenty-year career with you and at some point things begin to move down rather than up. We weren't having success with Ronnie in country or pop, and he felt like he wanted to move on too because we had a very heavy deal with several more albums to record. I sat down with him and said, "If we're going to continue, we cannot continue on the levels we are currently putting out albums on you."

Ronnie went to work with Jimmy Bowen at Capitol Records. Although Jimmy is one of Nashville's most experienced producers, success still eluded Ronnie. Then Ronnie signed with Warner Bros. Records but never had the kind of success he had had with RCA, but this fact did not diminish his talent. I think that one of the things some people miss is this: If we can understand the artist and understand what we can or cannot do for that artist, and if we are honest about it, some people just don't like that kind of honesty—but that honesty may be the reality. So, they moved on to other places, and that was their choice. I totally understand why that happens.

Waylon Jennings

Waylon was in my office a few days ago revisiting the old days. Waylon too has a fantastic sense of humor, and like Dolly and Ronnie he is a real person, true to himself. Waylon has the same great talent and fresh and original sense of humor as he had twenty years ago. I just recently heard his new record he recorded with Sheryl Crow and Sting and others. He still really rocks. He is a unique talent and a one-of-a-kind entertainer. We had a lot of number 1 records together, sold a lot of units, had a lot of fun, and broke a lot of records (no pun intended). I have many very fond memories about my days with Waylon.

When Waylon left RCA, I wasn't in Nashville. In 1990, I had returned to New York as the president of RCA Records; Thom Schuyler was in charge in my stead. But essentially the same scenario had taken place for Waylon as had taken place for Dolly and Ronnie. The label had reached a point where there was no place to go as far as more structures and deals. So Waylon moved on.

After all this time, it's wonderful to know that at any time I could pick up the phone and call Dolly, Waylon, or Ronnie, or they could call me, and it would be like old times. They are a part of my experiences and career. I will always be grateful to them for helping me learn the ropes.

Technology

It is so unfortunate that many people do not understand that the accomplishments of Waylon Jennings and Willie Nelson are a living history in the music industry. Waylon and Willie used to sell out Madison Square Garden and the Nassau Coliseum, which for country boys was probably one of the greatest accomplishments ever attained in the 1980s. They did it all without sound and lights, smashing guitars, or all the tricks of the trade that some country acts have borrowed from the rock 'n roll shows. They did it just playing their music. The people who showed up at their shows were politicians and movie stars. Willie and Waylon filled all of those seats by playing music honestly, and as far as I am concerned, they out sold anybody in modern times because we had no technology like SoundScan to tell us that we had just sold 100,000 units. We didn't know. We just shipped the records and didn't know how many sold until a couple of years later after all the returns were in.

We now create future history based on new technology called Sound-Scan, and BDS [Broadcast Data Systems, the computerized detection device that lets you know how many plays you have on a given radio station] is a techno-aid for SoundScan. Supertech has become the benchmark in deciding new history in the making. Technology is rewriting history. We have changed the criteria for how many units have to sell to make the product gold. We have more components. We used to have LPs. Now we have CDs, cassettes, and DRDs [double records]. These components did not exist back when Waylon and Willie were doing their music.

Bygone Times

Today, if any of these fine artists wanted to come back to RCA, I would say that that wouldn't be a good move for them or us. It's like having a first love end and years later to go back, only you cannot recapture that great chemistry you once had. That time has passed. I respect what all of them have done for the music industry, and I have only the best memories, but for them to subject themselves to today's music would be like watching a retired sports hero trying to play in today's games. This does not mean that they did not have a great twenty-year career. It does mean that today they would be competing against twenty-year-old artists, and that is a very difficult situation to be in.

One artist who would not accept the fact that he was not selling records was Charley Pride. He did not go gracefully. Everybody else who left the label understood, and we have remained friends. That was not the case in this situation. As far as I know, Charley is not on a label today.

I will make this statement for the entire music industry. When you look back, I wonder how many of today's artists will have the kind of legacy that Dolly Parton, Waylon Jennings, Ronnie Milsap, Tammy Wynette, Loretta Lynn, and Patsy Cline have had. When you look back on their catalogs, how many artists today, even if they sell five million albums, have that kind of legacy and that kind of total honesty in their music? At that time, we awarded artists for originality. Today, we don't reward them for that.

RCA and BNA: 1998

We have a total of fourteen artists on RCA and BNA Records. Originally, the reason for having two labels under one umbrella was to enable us to receive more airplay. Radio stations allow so much airtime per label. Today, having two labels allows us to take on a number of different projects and bring them into the marketplace. If, however, you have only one label, with two acts, then I have only two chances to break those acts. If I have two labels, I will have four or five chances to break through.

Signing Artists

For major corporations, budget is never a consideration in signing acts. Signing acts is contingent on how many artists we feel we can creatively handle and give enough attention to in order to move their careers forward.

In terms of the various artists who are signed to our companies, there is really no difference in the two labels. They're both country labels. People don't buy labels. They buy artists. Therefore, there does not need to be a difference in the labels. They're both country labels.

We have A&R people who go out, on a regular basis, to visit various showcases around the Nashville area. However, most of the time we will sign an artist from having received a tape of him singing. It might be just a simple tape, pitched by a songwriter who has hired a demo singer. When we hear the tape, if we like what we hear, we will find out more about the singer. Many times publishing houses hire demo singers. Then it's just a matter of us getting in touch with the publisher and perhaps arranging a meeting with the singer. Renee Bell, who is vice president of A&R, heard Jason Sellers and Sara Evans singing on demo tapes. Ultimately those tapes initiated their being signed to the label. Other major artists who started out as demo singers were Aaron Tippin, Garth Brooks, and Alan Jackson. A lot of artists begin as demo singers.

The main criteria at RCA for signing an artist, talent being a given, are their honesty and uniqueness. Dolly Parton was and is a completely honest person, as is Waylon Jennings. If you walk into the RCA building today, you will still see quotes by Waylon taken from various interviews he had given over the years. Waylon and Dolly talked openly and honestly about what they believed in and their childhood principles. Statements that come from someone's heart are always better than any prepackaged statements.

Advances

We give all of our artists advances. We don't ask if the money is for debts, living expenses, food, or whatever—that's their choice. Advances fluctuate between a low of $20,000 and a high of $50,000 over a one-year period of time. At the end of the year, each artist's career is reevaluated. Then it is decided how much their next advance should be. Sometimes the advance may be lower, sometimes higher, depending on individual contracts and the success of the artist. We continue to advance our artists until they are no longer with our label.

If the artist is also a songwriter, then he will also receive royalty payments from his performing rights organization for airplay. He will be paid by his publisher on mechanical sales. Also, the artist will receive a percentage of sales, after various expenses have been paid, from the label. If he is a new artist, he will receive anywhere from 10 to 15 percent of the sales after expenses.

We do charge the artist for recording costs and a portion of video costs. However, we do not charge the artist for promotion, advertising, showcases, photo sessions, and so on. We pay for a very large piece of the pie. If the artist does not make it, the company just absorbs the loss.

A&R

Our A&R department consists of myself, Renee Bell, and Sam Ramage. Basically, the A&R department makes the creative decisions regarding existing artists and also decides which artists will be signed to the label. But, all of our departments work together in deciding how to handle various aspects of an artist's career.

The Music

I think that country music has always been varied. For instance, Eddy Arnold sang both "Cattle Call" and "Make the World Go Away." Ronnie Milsap sang "I Hate You" and "There's No Gettin' over Me." Dolly Parton sang "A Coat of Many Colors" and "Here You Come Again." All of these artists sang songs with a great degree of variance as to genre.

Selecting songs for the artist depends on whether you have an artist who is completely in charge of his career and knows best what he should be singing or whether you have an artist whose songs are selected by a process of collaboration with the A&R department and the artist.

Radio

To me, promotion and sales are one and the same. Our sales and promotion staff call on radio stations in order to sell our product. We try to convince people that our product is the best product, and we explain the reasons why our product should receive airplay, be placed in record stores, receive media attention, and so on.

Radio stations do not have a set criteria as to how many times a day they can play a certain label's artist. Ten years ago, there were eight to ten record companies that dominated the radio playlists. At that point in time, there was a scenario where some dominant labels received all of the airplay. Creating several promotion staffs, under the same umbrella, enabled labels to get some of the marketing shares away from the competitive labels. This scenario was in place ten years ago. But, with every year that goes by, radio stations are becoming free marketplaces more than they ever were before. In the last few years, the subject of airplay per label is no longer a consideration. In general, a combination of the program director, the music director, and the general manager at radio stations make the decisions as to what records will be played. However, each individual radio station has their own way of deciding who will receive airplay.

When an artist receives airplay, public awareness, over a period of time, should increase sales for that artist's catalog of songs. It all depends on whether the listeners like that artist's songs. If they like them, they may buy the record. If they don't like the songs, they won't buy the record.

When you have an artist going into a particular venue to perform, you will want to make the public aware that your artist will be there. Then the radio station in that area will be contacted by people on our promotion staff in order to set up on-air interviews with the artist; we also make time buys so that the artist's records will be played more frequently during the dates of the performances. We may also put some kind of a public interest contest together, coordinating the contests with the artists being in that area, in order to enhance audience listening to that station. We also get spots added to the station in order to advertise the show and the product we are selling.

The Marketplace

I don't think that the labels are doing anything wrong regarding how the creative aspects of the artists and the material presented are handled. Realistically, today the marketplace is very difficult. The chances of being successful in this business are less than 5 percent. Fewer than one out of ten acts succeeds in being around for a few years. The consumer is the ultimate judge.

The A&R department and the artist decide what songs that artist will record. I think that if you get too many people involved in song selection it just creates confusion. At RCA we are very focused. There are very few people who are at the meeting when it is decided what songs are to be recorded. Also, depending on whether the artist's producer is active or passive, he may or may not have some input. The artist and the A&R people make the final decision.

Once the record is made, we try to lay out a strategy as a single sequence for the company. Then, if the company has an opinion that we think is valid, we'll try to reevaluate those opinions along with the artist, the A&R department, and the rest of the company executives. But we do not put the finished product out for bid. We stay focused on why we picked the songs and what our belief is in terms of the artist.

Even when the artist is out on the road promoting the new record, audience response to the songs does not change our collective mind as to the songs we chose for that artist and that artist's album. The way people react to a particular song during a live performance may be vastly different from the way they may react listening to the same song on the radio. But there are times when the artist's input as to audience response regarding a song may be valid. If an entire room stands up to applaud a song, consideration may be given to that material.

Everything is about listening. No matter what career you may pursue, you must listen. You need to understand what people are saying. This is a business of communication. What is the artist talking about in the lyric? What are the circumstances that create a given response to a song? What is the artist trying to convey? How does that artist see and present himself? Everything is about continually learning about relationships.

To any artist who comes into the label, I will say, "The more you get to know me, and the more I get to know you, the better the job I can do. If I understand you, if I can learn all that there is good about you and all there is about you that may be weak, I can do my best work. But if you hide your true self from me, I can't do my best work. I am here to facilitate your vision, your hopes, your dreams—that's what my job is."

Changes

If I could change the music industry, I would ask that label executives in New York and Los Angeles come to have a deeper and more realistic understanding of how Nashville's labels function. Parent companies open branch labels in Nashville with the unrealistic expectation that they will have a pot of gold at the end of the rainbow. However, what they are finding, at rainbow's end, is a pot of lucky charms. In order to get that pot of gold, careers had to have begun ten or fifteen years ago.

These unrealistic expectations raise the cost of doing business and make the marketplace overcrowded, and as a result their chances of obtaining that pot of gold have been greatly reduced. The home office executives will look at SoundScan and the trades and see that certain artists who have been around for a long time have sold enough product to have gold and platinum records. Therefore, they don't understand why other artists are not achieving like results. The fact is, regardless of economic structuring, there are very few who succeed in the music industry. If money were the solution, many artists would achieve great success rather than a few.

Cause and Effect

The country music boom started in 1988 and peaked in 1992. It was a whole lot easier to be successful than it is today. In the past, there was far less competition among the labels, and the marketplace was more open to various formats that they are no longer open to.

Certain business practices, in my opinion, have not been good for the industry. For instance, when a record company underprices its product in order to obtain record sales, that hurts the rest of the industry that is keeping its prices in line with current market values and trends. RCA would not undercut product price for an artist in order to ensure an unrealistic accounting of sales based on reduced CD and cassette prices. Why a label would allow an artist's product to be sold at greatly reduced prices, I do not know. When a company sells a 24-song CD or cassette for $13, when market value for a 10- or 12-song product should be $16, this causes product devaluation for the entire industry. I do believe that 90 percent of the record company executives in Nashville would agree that this practice is lowering the cost of the value of the product, and this practice only serves the individual, not the industry.

One reason the music industry is in a slump is because the music is not as fresh, imaginative, and creative as it once was. There are too many followers and not enough leaders, both in radio and at the labels. People are afraid to take chances with something new.

RCA tries to find artists who are great singers, not just good singers; we're making records that are different. We're trying to build albums and careers. Anyone who takes a look at Martina McBride, Alabama, Kenny Chesney, and Sara Evans knows that our company's standards are very high. RLG builds artists. That is what our history is, and that is what we will continue to do, and that is what my focus is.

In 1998, sales were down dramatically for some artists who have been around for a number of years. However, radio continues to play their product. I have seen this happen before, where artists who were once at the top of the trade charts are no longer selling records. Radio is not leading; it is following. Radio executives do not feel the changes in the industry as quickly as do label executives. We see the changes because, every day, we see the sales figures. For example, radio could continue to play an RCA record every day for twenty years if that particular artist is a successful act in the minds of the radio executives, but that does not mean that the public is still buying that artist's product. Labels are very aware of products that are no longer selling. However, radio tends to give a greater value to certain artists than do the labels, primarily because radio does not see the sales figures. Also, radio is not as aware of the drop in concert ticket sales as the labels are. When products are no longer selling and people are no longer buying concert tickets, then it is time for a change. But, unfortunately, many people do not like change, and they try to hold on to what once worked in the past rather than moving forward and taking chances with new artists. We are paid to take chances, and hopefully we are right more often than we are wrong.

There is an evolution or cycle that occurs naturally, if left alone, whereby artists who are no longer selling and whose careers have peaked are no longer played. There is no room for new artists to have a shot at rising to the top as long as the older artists and radio are not allowing the new artists to have their well-deserved chance. Eventually, sales reach such a nadir that change occurs, but when that occurs, I have no idea. In the meantime, the entire industry suffers in a stalemate situation until the new artists finally get their shot at the success that the older artists have already had.

Options

As a music industry executive, I try to listen to as much music as I possibly can, both inside the country format and outside of that format. There are a lot of options out there today. It's a daunting task to keep up with all of the new music, to be on top of changing cultural trends on television, to have a firm idea of new tastes, to know who the relevant stars are, to be informed about all that is going on with motion pictures, to have a good understanding of current books, to understand fashion trends, and so on. To do all that is thought to be necessary of you, and to fulfill all of your executive obligations, at times, takes a superman.

Choices

Sometimes the public will buy the song but will not buy the act. An example of this is Billy Ray Cyrus's "Achy Breaky Heart." The song sold, but the act did not sell.

A hit for a publisher is based on what percentage of the publishing he owns in order to generate performance income. A hit for an agent may be defined as a Top 10 record, whereby the agent can then justify raising his fees. A hit for a label is always based on units sold. We do not look at box office ticket sales, publishing, or merchandise sold—we only look at sales.

Today, the public has many options both in and out of the country music format and the music industry. The competition is tremendous and varied, ranging from musical formats such as rap, pop, alternative, R&B, soft rock, hard rock, heavy metal, and so on, to video games, the World Wide Web, the Internet, theme parks, cable television, movies, and a multitude of available, affordable, and accessible hobbies.

There is nothing new or surprising when you look at the country charts in the trades. The same choices or lack of choices are right there in the Top 10—Reba McEntire, George Strait, Garth Brooks, Shania Twain—where too many want them to be. However, if you look at the pop charts, you'll see forty names that you never heard of before—new, fresh, and exciting talent. The country format is far too narrow. There are several acts that do most of the ticket sales, have a certain majority of the record sales, and have the largest number of songs in a radio station's library. In other formats, there is a lot more mystery about what is happening in the industry.

I've heard that adults don't like change or new information. But I'm an adult, and I see a different movie every week, I watch a tremendous range of programs on television, and my record collection is in the hundreds. If you peek into cars in a parking lot, you will often see half a dozen CDs or cassettes lying around, not just one and not just the same acts. I think adults prefer change. I don't know why the country format is so narrow. I can't answer that question. I would equate our industry format to having one player on a major sports team who does everything, which may be great to pull the team up for a season; but if the rest of the team never comes together, what do you do? Our business, for the last several years, has been like that. There will be the same few acts who will put out two or three new projects, which will, for a season, make the country music industry look as though it is successful. What happens when an entire industry is dependent on a few acts? What happens next year if those few acts don't deliver? What happens is that the entire industry goes into a deep slump.

The quality in our industry needs to improve both at the executive level and at the creative level.

Autonomy and Interest

Executives, whether foreign or domestic, do not come to Nashville and dictate who should be signed to a label. That does not happen.

I worked in New York. Most people who are from New York or Los Angeles don't like to come to Nashville. This fact is obvious by the number of executives who come to Nashville for the Country Music Association awards show or the Academy of Country Music show. Maybe one or two executives will come to town from time to time, but they do not come to Nashville on a regular basis. However, executives go to the Grammy awards or the Rock 'n Roll Hall of Fame awards in great numbers because that is where they feel the most comfortable.

In Nashville, we only have one format: country radio. So, if you're able to be successful here, given this narrow format, I believe you will have an excellent foundation and working knowledge of the music industry as a whole. I think that any time you can network and intermingle on the idea side, it helps. Aside from a depth of knowledge and a communicative exchange of ideas, I still don't know if radio, country music television, and the record industry are all on the same page, as in, "Listen, guys and girls, we have a problem. We are not growing in audience numbers. And, if we stay this way, we will continue to have too much supply for way too little demand, and something's got to give."

Pretty People

Our society, in general, rewards pretty people. All you have to do is look at all of the new nighttime soaps. You can't tell me that most of these people are wonderful and accomplished actors and actresses. Today, we look at the covers of national magazines and define beauty as being physically fit and trendy. We are taught to envy those people, to aspire to become like them, to become their fans. This is also true in music videos—it's just a sign of the times.

Our culture has changed greatly over the years. For better or worse, I believe that it is vitally important that our society, which is guided in part by our artists and our music, be given choices based on creative quality, mystery, excitement, and change.

Country Music

Country music has not changed much over the years. The lyrics address problems that everyday people run into on a daily basis. They tend to focus on real-life emotional scenarios that adult or young adult people are involved in.

Alternative music and urban music lend themselves more to a feel, an emotional aspiration, or a groove, while country music is more lyric driven. Country music's format is narrow in terms of artists, not in terms of songs. There are approximately seven acts that occupy more than their proportionate share of space on radio. We're narrow in terms of the artists because the stars represent too much weight in our format.

RLG

RLG tries to find artists who are identifiable and unique from a personality standpoint and a vocal standpoint. Our artists separate themselves from other artists when you listen to the radio. We want our listeners to have a clear and accurate picture of who they are hearing, visualizing, and identifying with. As long as I am here, I will always be looking for something new, different, challenging, and exciting.

Epilogue

The goal of record labels, no matter which kind of music they record, is the same: to sell their products to the public. As all the record executives presented here attest, selling their products continues to be a challenge. Independent labels are becoming more scarce, multinational parent companies are the norm, and consolidation often makes it more difficult for artists and technicians to find a place in the music business.

The record executives interviewed in this book provide some clues, however, to breaking into the tightly knit country music community—into record labels, publishing houses, and managers' offices. No one will spoon-feed the newcomer: Years of dues must be paid, and newcomers must learn by observation, joining professional organizations, and networking at the industry functions.

Most of all, an aspiring artist or technician must be patient and have the right attitude. While talent is important, a good personality is just as critical, and often more difficult to come by. Professionals in the music industry know that a person can be taught how to write through mentoring, given voice lessons to improve his range and delivery, placed with a publicist to give him media exposure, and even put on a diet to change his appearance. But no one can give a person the humility and attitude needed to be a success. No one gets anywhere by being pushy and aggressive, and once inappropriate behavior is displayed, a second chance is rarely given.

This can be a problem for artists who rise too quickly. Early success can give an artist the false impression that he is better than he is. He may become self-important and think he got where he is by himself. A bad attitude can cause professionals who started out with him to no longer want to work with him. If he's attained enough fame by the time he shows his true colors, public loyalty may keep him selling records and in the game, though Nashville insiders will have nothing more to do with him. If he hasn't gained the status to be self-propellant, he will fall by the wayside and never be heard from again.

This is where dues-paying can be helpful. An artist who spends years paying dues will learn to appreciate how competitive the industry is and how fortunate he is just to have a meeting with a label executive. He's more likely to have the right attitude and to appreciate the expert help of producers, managers, publicists, cowriters, A&R people, session musicians, studio engineers, and the many others who make a career in music possible. This is the most typical means to success—the legendary overnight success is largely a myth.

While the Nashville music industry is difficult to break into, skill and hard-working, humble attitudes will give aspiring artists, technicians, and "record men" the best chance of enduring success—of achieving an enduring place in Nashville like that attained by the talented label executives featured here.

Glossary

Advances—Monies paid out by the record labels to producers and artists. These advances are recouped by the record label from future record sales.

Album Cut—A song on any given album, CD, or cassette that has not been designated to receive airplay.

Airplay—When a song is played on the radio. Writers and publishers are paid for airplay by their performing rights organization.

ASCAP—Acronym for the American Society of Composers, Authors and Publishers, a performing rights organization.

"A"-side—The side that is shipped to all major reporting radio stations. It is the side that has been chosen to receive airplay by the record label executives.

BMI—Acronym for Broadcast Music Incorporated, a performing rights organization.

Billboard—A major trade magazine in the music industry. It contains lists of charts that indicate airplay and sales.

Blue Bird Cafe—A Nashville nightspot where many famous artists have performed prior to and after being signed to major record label deals. It is also well known for its writers' nights, where both amateur and professional writers entertain the patrons on preappointed nights.

Classic—A song that has been recorded many times by the original artist. An example of a classic song is, "Don't It Make My Brown Eyes Blue," recorded by Crystal Gayle and written by Richard Leigh.

Cut—When a song is cut, it has been recorded.

Dead in the Can—A term used for songs recorded in a studio that ultimately did not get released on the album. When the publishing on those songs has already been signed away, the material is said to be "dead in the can." It may get released at a later date, but usually the publishing would have to be negotiated. The "can" is the metal container used to store tapes.

Demo—Short for demonstration. A demo tape is a tape containing from three to five original songs. The songwriters make demo tapes to give to various industry professionals in order to get their songs recorded.

Draws—Monies paid out to the artist by the record label and later recouped by the artist's label from future record sales. Draws are also paid out to signed staff writers. Their draws are recouped by their publishing house, prior to paying the writers, from their future royalty checks. A staff writer's draw may range from between $50 to $500 a week, depending on that writer's past successes.

Laid Down—When sound (meaning instruments and vocals) is laid down, it has been recorded.

Mastered—The completion of all of the tracks on a project for a recording artist. Usually, because of the high cost of a major recording session, only major artists who are signed to record companies that are picking up the tab can afford a professionally mastered session. (Studio time in Nashville on master sessions can run upwards of $2,500 a day, and a completed project may cost as much as $250,000.)

Mechanical License—A licensing agreement between the copyright holder and the user of the material. If a producer wants to use a certain song for a movie soundtrack, he must first pay for and obtain a mechanical license from the legal owner of the song's copyright, which may be the writer and/or the publisher.

Mechanical Royalties—Royalties paid to songwriters every six months by the publisher they have signed a publishing contract with on a particular song. A mechanical unit is a mechanism manufactured to produce sound recordings. These mechanisms are either CDs or cassettes. Every writer and publisher who has an interest in any given song receives, according to their individual contracts, a percentage of anywhere from 10 to 50 percent of the net profits per unit sold. For example, although contracts are as individual as the writers and publishers, if a unit grosses for $16.95, after expenses are deducted—

which may include payment back to the label for artwork, pressing, mailing, advances, publicity, promotion, and so on—the writers' and publishers' percentages are taken out of the net amount, which may be around $7. Therefore the publisher and the writer may receive anywhere from 70¢ to $3.50 per unit sold, respectively. If there is more than one writer on the song, then the writers' net percentage is split evenly between the writers. If there is more than one publisher on the song, then the publishers' net percentage is split evenly between the publishers. Many units must be sold to make any money from mechanical payments. Airplay monies are paid, as previously mentioned, by the writer's and/or publisher's performing rights organization—ASCAP, BMI, or SESAC.

Mix—The arrangement and the final production and polishing techniques on a project. Usually the producer, artist, studio engineer, and other involved persons on an artist's project decide exactly how they want the music to sound. They decide which instruments should be given more volume or less volume, how the vocal arrangements should be done, when the turnarounds and instrumental breaks should take place, and so on. A mix is done after all of the tracks on a project have been laid down.

Personal Manager—A manager who works for the artist and coordinates the artist's schedules with producers, record label executives, publicists, video producers, booking agents, photographers, and so on. Personal managers oversee the contracts their artists negotiate with various entities in the industry.

Performing rights organization—An organization that pays writers and publishers who are affiliates when a song they have an interest in receives radio airplay, is performed in concert, is performed on television, or is performed in a motion picture. Writers and publishers usually belong to at least one of the three major performing rights organizations, ASCAP, BMI, and SESAC. A publisher may belong to one or all three affiliations. A writer may belong only to one affiliation. The reason that major publishing houses belong to all three affiliations is because they have signed staff writers who belong to different affiliations. For example, out of a staff of 100 songwriters, perhaps 50 will be affiliated with ASCAP, 30 with BMI, and 20 may be affiliated with SESAC. The publisher must have active publishing contracts with the writer's affiliation in order to publish and clear that writer's song through their respective affiliation, so as to receive payment from that affiliation. A songwriter may have only one affiliation collecting monies for him.

Points—A term used by performing rights organizations. Each point equates to a specific amount of money. For example, one point may be worth anywhere from 10¢ to $2, depending what time of day and how much airplay a certain song has received. The money amount for each point continually varies because the performing rights organizations conform with the national economy at the time of performance of each song. If the national economy is doing well, the points will be worth more per point. If the national economy is not doing well, the points will reflect the slump. Points are computed by a worldwide computer network. This is a hit-and-miss network—in other words, the computers will pick up tallies from different reporting radio stations each pay cycle. The points are tallied up to determine how much the writers and publishers will be paid for having their songs played on the more than 2,500 United States reporting radio stations, as well as all of their overseas affiliates.

R&R—A major trade magazine in the music industry. *R&R* [*Radio & Record*] contains charts that indicate how much airplay a song has received.

Rack Jobber—Someone who ensures that a designated number of cassettes and CDs are on a store's racks.

Record Guys—The record label executives who take care of the business side of the business. They oversee all departments within their label and make sure that all accounts and budgets are properly handled.

Reporting Stations—Those major radio stations that report how much airplay a certain song has received to the three performing rights organizations, ASCAP, BMI, and SESAC.

SESAC—Originally an acronym for the Society of European Stage Authors and Composers, today only used in acronym form. One of the three major performing rights organizations.

Side—One song. If an album, CD, or cassette contains ten sides, that album contains ten songs.

Singles—Those songs that receive airplay.

Spec—Short for the word speculation.

Standard Song—A song that has been recorded by many different artists. An example of a standard song is "Jingle Bells."

Tracking—Musical tracks laid down during the master session. Tracking is done in the studio by the studio engineers and the producer on the session. Within the studio is a huge board, the cost of which may exceed $250,000. In major recording studios, these boards are equipped with thirty-six to forty-eight tracks. Each track, which may be visualized as one cassette tape, is used for each instrument. For example, the session drummer may play several drums on one session, a track is needed for each drum: the snare, bass, tom-tom, treble, kick drum, cymbals, percussion instruments, and so on; the drummer may easily use up eight tracks. Other tracks are used by musicians on: lead guitar, rhythm guitar, piano [full sounding keys], keyboard [light sounding keys], violins, and horns; more tracks are needed for individual instrumental harmony tracks. Tracks are also used for the recording artist's vocals and harmonies. (Each individual harmony must have a separate track. If the recording artist overdubs his own vocals with three-part harmony, then three tracks will be needed). Background vocals and special effects (like the sound of thunder or rain) also need their own tracks. It doesn't take long to use all forty-eight tracks. In all major recording sessions, the session musicians lay down the instrumental tracks first; then, at a later date, the artist will come into the studio and sing his vocal tracks; then his vocals will be dubbed onto the instrumental tracks.

Unit—One CD or cassette.

Writers' Nights—Advertised and designated nights that are held in various area clubs in order to publicize songwriters and their songs. A great deal of industry networking takes place at writers' nights, and tourists as well as local residents and industry professionals take advantage of the good food and fine music offered during these get-togethers.

Bibliography

Business

Jennings, Waylon, and Lenny Kaye. *Waylon: An Autobiography.* Warner Books: New York, 1996.

Killen, Buddy, with Tom Carter. *By the Seat of My Pants.* Simon & Schuster: New York, 1993.

Pierce, Jennifer Ember. *Breakin' into Nashville: How to Write and Sell Country Music.* Madison Books: Lanham, Md., 1998.

Pierce, Jennifer Ember. *Playin' Around: The Lives and Careers of Famous Session Musicians.* Scarecrow Press: Lanham, Md., 1998.

Shemel, Sidney, and M. William Krasilovsky. *This Business of Music: A Practical Guide to the Music Industry for Publishers, Writers, Record Companies, Producers, Artists, Agents.* Billboard Publications: New York, 1985.

Trades

Billboard magazine, 1515 Broadway, New York, New York 10036, (212) 764-7300; 49 Music Square West, Nashville, Tennessee 37203; (615) 321-4290.

Close-Up magazine, (a CMA publication), One Music Circle South, Nashville, Tennessee 37203; (615) 244-2840.

Gavin magazine, 140 2nd Street, San Francisco, California 94150; (415) 459-1990.

Mix bookshelf, 6400 Hollis Street, Suite 12, Emeryville, California 94608; (800) 233-9604.

Music City News magazine, 50 Music Square West, Nashville, Tennessee 37203; (615) 329-2200.

Music Row magazine, P.O. Box 158542, Nashville, Tennessee 37215; (615) 321-3617.

Musician magazine, 1515 Broadway, New York, New York 10036; (212) 764-7300.

Radio & Record magazine, 1106 16th Avenue South, Nashville, Tennessee 37212; (615) 244-8822; 10100 Santa Monica Boulevard, Fifth Floor, Los Angeles, California 90067; (310) 553-4330.

List of Addresses

Music Associations, Affiliations, and Organizations

ACM
Academy of Country Music
6255 Sunset Boulevard
Suite 923
Hollywood, California 90028
(213) 462-2351

ASCAP
American Society of Composers,
Authors and Publishers
One Lincoln Plaza
New York, New York 10023
(800) 952-7227

Two Music Square West
Nashville, Tennessee 37203
(615) 742-5000

BMI
Broadcast Music, Inc.
320 West 56th Street
New York, New York 10019

10 Music Square East
Nashville, Tennessee 37203
(615) 401-2000

CMA
Country Music Association
One Music Circle South
Nashville, Tennessee 37203
(615) 244-2840

NARAS
National Academy of Recording
   Arts and Sciences
3402 Pico Boulevard
Santa Monica, California 90405
(310) 392-3777

1007 17th Avenue South
P.O. Box 121948
Nashville, Tennessee 37212
(615) 327-4308

SESAC
421 West 54th Street
New York, New York 10019-4450
(212) 486-3450

55 Music Square East
Nashville, Tennessee
(615) 320-0055

Record Labels

Aaron Records
P.O. Box 428
Portland, Tennessee 37148
(615) 325-3340
fax: (615) 325-5411

Arista Records
7 Music Circle North
Nashville, Tennessee 37203
(615) 780-9100
fax: (615) 780-9190

Asylum Records
1906 Acklen Avenue
Nashville, Tennessee 37212
(615) 292-7990
fax: (615) 292-8219

Atlantic Records
1812 Broadway
Nashville, Tennessee 37203
(615) 327-9394
fax: (615) 329-2008

Capitol Records/Nashville
3322 West End Avenue
11th Floor
Nashville, Tennessee 37203
(615) 269-2000
fax: (615) 269-2034

Columbia Records/Nashville
34 Music Square East
Nashville, Tennessee 37203
(615) 742-4358
fax: (615) 742-5741

Curb Records/MCG Curb
47 Music Square East
Nashville, Tennessee 37203
(615) 321-5080
fax: (615) 327-1964

Curb/Universal Records
43 Music Square East
Nashville, Tennessee 37203
(615) 742-3332
fax: (615) 255-2855

Dead Reckoning Records
P.O. Box 159178
Nashville, Tennessee 37215
(615) 292-7773
fax: (615) 383-9571

DreamWorks
1516 16th Avenue South
Nashville, Tennessee 37212
(615) 463-4600
fax: (615) 463-4601

Elektra Entertainment
75 Rockefeller Plaza
New York, New York 10019
(212) 275-4000

Giant Records
1514 South Street
Nashville, Tennessee 37212
(615) 256-3110
fax: (615) 259-4011

Heartland Records
575 Lexington Avenue
New York, New York 10022
(212) 753-4410
fax: (212) 753-4817

Intersound Country
1227 16th Avenue South
Nashville, Tennessee 37212
(615) 327-0770
Fax: (615) 327-1214

Justice Records
P.O. Box 980369
Houston, Texas 77098
(713) 520-6669
fax: (713) 525-4444

Lyric Street Records
824 19th Avenue South
Nashville, Tennessee 37203
(615) 963-4848
fax: (615) 963-4846

MCA Records/Nashville
60 Music Square East
Nashville, Tennessee 37203
(615) 244-8944
fax: (615) 880-7475

Mercury Records/Nashville
66 Music Square West
Nashville, Tennessee 37203
(615) 320-0110
fax: (615) 327-4856

Oh Boy Records
4121 Wilshire Boulevard
Suite 204
Los Angeles, California 90010
(213) 385-0082

RLG/Nashville (RCA Record
   Label Group)
One Music Circle North
Nashville, Tennessee 37203
(615) 664-1200
fax: (615) 664-1226

Reprise Records/Nashville
20 Music Square East
Nashville, Tennessee 37203
(615) 214-1500
fax: (615) 214-1545

River North/Nashville
1227 16th Avenue South
Nashville, Tennessee 37212
(615) 327-0770
fax: (615) 327-0011

Rounder Records
1 Camp Street
Cambridge, Massachusetts
   02140
(617) 354-0700
fax: (617) 491-1970

Skaggs Family Records
54 Music Square East
Suite 301
Nashville, Tennessee 37203
(615) 255-4563
fax: (615) 248-6300

Sony Labels
(Columbia, Epic, Lucky Dog, and
   Monument Records)
34 Music Square East
Nashville, Tennessee
(615) 742-4321
fax: (615) 254-3879

Step One Records
1300 Division Street
Third Floor
Nashville, Tennessee 37203
(615) 255-3009
fax: (615) 255-6282

Sugar Hill Records
P.O. Box 55300
Durham, North Carolina
   27717-5300
(919) 489-4349
fax: (919) 489-6080

Virgin/Nashville
48 Music Square East
Nashville, Tennessee 37203
(615) 251-1100
fax: (615) 313-3700

Warner Bros. Records
20 Music Square East
Nashville, Tennessee 37203

(615) 748-8000
fax: (615) 214-1567

Word Records
3319 West End Avenue
Suite 200
Nashville, Tennessee 37203
(615) 457-1500

Record Labels and Artists

Aaron Records
Vicki Bird

Arista Records
Sherrie Austin
BlackHawk
BR5-49
Brooks & Dunn
Shannon Brown
Jim Collins
Clint Daniels
Diamond Rio
Little Jimmy Dickens
Radney Foster
Alan Jackson
Waylon Jennings
Brad Paisley
Lee Roy Parnell
Dolly Partin
Pam Tillis
Michelle Wright

Asylum Records
Chad Austin
Cox Family
Billy Crash Craddock
Melodie Crittenden
Rodney Crowell
George Jones

Noah Kelly
Kentucky HeadHunters
Lila McCann
Jennifer McCarter
Delbert McClinton
Mark Nessler
Bryan White

Atlantic Records
Confederate Railroad
John Conlee
Matt King
Tracy Lawrence
Neal McCoy
John Michael Montgomery

Capitol Records/Nashville
Trace Adkins
Rhett Akins
Susan Ashton
Asleep at the Wheel
Garth Brooks
Deana Carter
Delevantes (The)
Chris LeDoux
Brenda Lee
George Lindsey
Keith Urban
Leroy Van Dyke

Ricky Van Shelton
Steve Wariner

Curb Records/MCG Curb
Deborah Allen
Rodney Atkins
Blake and Brian
Junior Brown
Jeff Carson
Carlene Carter
Philip Claypool
David Kersh
Hal Ketchum
Tim McGraw
Ken Mellons
Jo Dee Messina
Perfect Stranger
LeAnn Rimes
Sawyer Brown
Trini Triggs
Tamara Walker
Hank Williams Jr.

Curb/Universal Records
Cactus Choir
Glen Campbell
Lyle Lovett
Shane McAnally
Seminole
Kevin Sharp
Wynonna

Dead Reckoning
Bluebloods (The)
Suzy Bogguss
James Bonamy
Dead Reckoners (The)
Billy Dean
Mike Henderson
Kieran Kane
Robert Earl Keen
Tammy Rogers

Kevin Welch
Kitty Wells

DreamWorks
Jessica Andrews
Lisa Angelle
Linda Davis
Mac Davis
Jeff Foxworthy
Janie Fricke
Mac McAnally
Redmon and Vale
Jerry Reed
Randy Travis
Darryl Worley

Elektra Entertainment
Jimmie Dale Gilmore
Jim Glasser
Nanci Griffith

Giant Records
Rebekah Del Rio
Terry McMillan
Clay Walker
Wilkinsons (The)
Don Williams

Heartland Records
Loretta Lynn
Shelby Lynne

Justice Records
Kris Kristofferson

Lyric Street Records
John Berry
Sonya Issacs
SheDaisy
Aaron Tippin
Lari White

MCA Records/Nashville
Gary Allen
Tracy Byrd
Alecia Elliot
Mark Chestnutt
Joe Ely
Ralph Emery
Ty England
Vince Gill
Keith Harling
Emmylou Harris
Freddie Hart
Reba McEntire
Allison Moorer
David Lee Murphy
Olivia Newton-John
Nitty Gritty Dirt Band
Ray Stevens
Doug Stone
George Strait
Marty Stuart
Doug Supernaw
Lee Ann Womack
Chely Wright
Michelle Wright
Trisha Yearwood

Mercury Records/Nashville
Terri Clark
Neal Coty
Billy Ray Cyrus
Lacy J. Dalton
Tom T. Hall
Eric Heatherly
Toby Keith
Sammy Kershaw
Kathy Mattea
Shane Minor
Kim Richey
Statler Brothers (The)
Keith Stegall
William Topley

Shania Twain
Mark Wills

Oh Boy Records
John Prine
Boots Randolph
Eddy Raven

Platinum Records/Nashville
Lynn Anderson
Banjomania
Bobby Bare
Bellamy Brothers (The)
Tim Briggs
T. Graham Brown
Earl Thomas Conley
Gatlin Brothers (The)
Crystal Gayle
Michael Johnson
Ronnie McDowell
Billy Joe Royal
Jo-El Sonnier

RLG/Nashville (RCA Record Label Group) RCA Records
Alabama
Eddy Arnold
Clint Black
Sara Evans
Don Everly
Skip Ewing
Donna Fargo
Narvel Feltz
Forester Sisters (The)
Keith Gattis
Andy Griggs
Merle Haggard
Martina McBride
Thompson Brothers Band (The)
Hank Thompson
Mel Tillis
Warren Brothers (The)

BNA Records
Kenny Chesney
Jennifer Day
Jim Lauderdale
Lonestar
Charlie Louvin
Mindy McCready
Mel McDaniel
Lorrie Morgan
Gary Morris
K. T. Oslin
Marie Osmond
Paul Overstreet
Jason Sellers
Ray Vega
Porter Wagoner

Reprise Records/Nashville
Bill Anderson
John Anderson
Paul Brandt
Lynns (The)
Charlie Major
Barbara Mandrell
Irlene Mandrell
Louise Mandrell
Michael Peterson
Randy Scruggs
Dwight Yoakam

River North/Nashville
Juice Newton

Rounder Records
Alison Krauss and Union Station
Jim and Jesse
Cledus T. Judd
Riders In The Sky (The)
Jeannie C. Riley

Skaggs Family Records
Ricky Skaggs

Sony Labels (Columbia, Epic, Lucky Dog, and Monument Records) Columbia Records
Chet Atkins
Lisa Brokop
Mary Chapin Carpenter
Deryl Dodd
Wade Hayes
Killer Beaz
Montgomery/Gentry
Ricochet
Earl Scruggs
Rick Trevino

Epic Records
Joe Diffie
Ty Herndon
Highway 101
Kinleys (The)
Patty Loveless
Shana Petrone
Ray Price
Charley Pride
Collin Raye
Sons of the Desert

Lucky Dog Records
David Allan Coe
Mark Collie
Jack Ingram
Johnny Paycheck

Monument Records
Dixie Chicks (The)
Gil Grand
Yankee Grey

Step One Records
Jack Greene
Lee Greenwood
Gene Watson
Western Flyer
Whites (The)

Sugar Hill Records
Jerry Douglas
Holly Dunn
Nashville Bluegrass Band (The)
Tim O'Brien
Oak Ridge Boys (The)
Sweethearts of the Rodeo (The)
Doc Watson

Virgin Records
Roy D. Mercer
Julie Reeves
River Road
Johnny Rodriguez

Warner Bros. Records
David Ball
Chad Brock
Claudia Church
Roy Clark

Anita Cochran
Chris Cummings
Don Edwards
Bill Engvall
Faith Hill
Lace
Bill Miller
Ronnie Milsap
Waddie Mitchell
Brady Seals
Dan Seals
Connie Smith
Karen Staley
Red Stegall
Travis Tritt
Tanya Tucker

Word Records
George Hamilton IV

Publicists

Alabama HQ
101 Glen Boulevard
Fort Payne, Alabama 35967
(205) 845-4283
fax: (205) 845-7780

Aristo Media
P.O. Box 22765
Nashville, Tennessee 37202
(615) 269-7071
fax: (615) 269-0131

Alison Auerbach Public Relations
1229 17th Avenue South
Nashville, Tennessee 37212
(615) 329-0025
fax: (615) (615) 329-0403

The Baker/Northrop Media Group
13351-D Riverside Drive
Suite 611
Sherman Oaks, California 91423
(818) 501-0056
fax: (818) 501-0068

Bender, Goldman and Halper
1500 West Olympic Boulevard
Suite 655
Los Angeles, California 90064
(310) 473-4147
fax: (310) 473-0476

The Brokaw Company
9255 Sunset Boulevard
Suite 804
Los Angeles, California 90069

(310) 273-2060
fax: (310) 276-4037

The Brokaw Company
1915 Church Street
Nashville, Tennessee 37203
(615) 329-9360
fax: (615) 329-9647

CDB, Inc.
17060 Central Pike
Lebanon, Tennessee 37087
(615) 443-2112
fax: (615) 443-3140

Susan Collier Public Relations
6204 Jocelyn Hollow Road
Nashville, Tennessee 37205
(615) 356-0375
fax: (615) 352-7829

Dassinger Creative Services
32 Ardsley
Suite 201
Montclair, New Jersey 07042
(201) 746-6474
fax: (201) 746-5082

Bob Doyle and Associates
1111 17th Avenue South
Nashville, Tennessee 37212
(615) 329-1040
fax: (615) 329-1021

Crabtree Public Relations
118 16th Avenue South
Suite 219
Nashville, Tennessee 37203
(615) 255-7225
fax: (615) 259-4011

Force, Inc.
1505 16th Avenue South

Nashville, Tennessee 37212
(615) 385-4646
fax: (615) 385-5840

Front Page Publicity
P.O. Box 681828
Franklin, Tennessee 37068
(615) 591-2442
fax: (615) 591-2661

Greg Fowler Promotions
201 Glenn Avenue Southwest
Fort Payne, Alabama 35967
(205) 845-4283
fax: (205) 845-7780

Full Court Press
437 2nd Avenue South
Nashville, Tennessee 37201
(615) 254-7224
fax: (615) 254-1120

Full Moon Entertainment
P.O. Box 2437
Hendersonville, Tennessee 37077
(615) 824-1688
fax: (615) 824-0640

GB Management
1111 17th Avenue South
Nashville, Tennessee 37212
(615) 329-0166
fax: (615) 329-9470

Kathy Gangwisch and Associates
207 Westport Road
Kansas City, Missouri 64111
(816) 931-8000
fax: (816) 931-0289

Gurley and Company
P.O. Box 150657

Nashville, Tennessee 37215
(615) 269-0474
fax: (615) 385-2052

Lana Higgins PR
P.O. Box 943
Madison, Tennessee 37116
(615) 223-1798
(no fax listed)

Margy Holland
111 Academy Square
Nashville, Tennessee 37210
(615) 248-4009
fax: (615) 731-3005

Holley and Harman Public
   Relations
3415 West End Avenue
Suite 101G
Nashville, Tennessee
(615) 460-9550
fax: (615) 460-9553

Hot Schatz Productions
P.O. Box 50221
Nashville, Tennessee 37205
(615) 356-6614
fax: (615) 356-8594

Joe's Garage
4405 Belmont Park Terrace
Nashville, Tennessee 37215
(615) 269-3238
fax: (615) 297-7612

Kaleidoscope Media
8032-1/2 West Norton Avenue
West Hollywood, California
   90046
(213) 654-5453
(no fax listed)

Little Horn Communications
3108 Stoneybrook Road
Oklahoma City, Oklahoma 73120
(405) 755-8288
fax: (405) 755-8292

Network Ink
2021 21st Avenue South
Nashville, Tennessee 37221
(615) 297-0550
fax: (615) 383-2349

PLA Media
1303 16th Avenue South
Nashville, Tennessee 37212
(615) 327-0100
fax: (615) 320-1061

PMK Media
955 South Carrillo
Suite 200
Los Angeles, California 90048
(213) 954-4000
fax: (213) 954-4011

The Press Office
1229 17th Avenue South
Nashville, Tennessee 37212
(615) 320-5153
fax: (615) 320-5738

Ellen Pryor
3811 Rolland Road
Nashville, Tennessee 37205
(615) 292-8297
fax: (615) 297-5168

Robers and Cowan
1888 Century Park East
5th Floor
Los Angeles, California 90067
(310) 201-8800
fax: (310) 557-2816

Rubin Media
P.O. Box 158161
Nashville, Tennessee 37215
(615) 320-5000
fax: (615) 320-5551

Schmidt Relations
411 Newberry Court
Goodlettsville, Tennessee 37072
(615) 851-3878
fax: (615) 851-4878

The Mitch Schneider Organization
14724 Ventura Boulevard
Suite 410
Sherman Oaks, California 91403
(818) 380-0400
fax: (818) 380-0430

Evelyn Shriver Public Relations
9 Music Square West
Nashville, Tennessee 37203
(615) 782-0078
fax: (615) 782-0088

So Much Moore
P.O. Box 120426
Nashville, Tennessee 37212
(615) 298-1689
fax: (615) 298-1446

Starkeeper Public Relations
P.O. Box 128195
Nashville, Tennessee 37212

(615) 329-0460
fax: (615) 329-0416

Starstruck Entertainment
40 Music Square West
Nashville, Tennessee 37203
(615) 259-0001
fax: (615) 259-5222

Trifecta Entertainment
209 10th Avenue South
Suite 302
Nashville, Tennessee 37203
(615) 254-3333
fax: (615) 254-5472

Turner and Company
1018 17th Avenue South
Suite 6
Nashville, Tennessee 37212
(615) 327-1274
fax: (615) 322-9462

K. West Company
P.O. Box 24545
Nashville, Tennessee 37202
(615) 383-9388
fax: (615) 383-6294

White Horse Enterprises
P.O. Box 90751
Nashville, Tennessee 37209
(615) 350-8970
fax: (615) 350-8938

Index

157

Blue Hat, xxiii
BNA (Berry Field/Nashville Airport)
   Records, xxi, xxiii, 27, 92, 116, 118,
   119, 128–36
Bogguss, Suzy, 50
Boone, Debby, 55, 107, 108, 110
Bowen, Jimmy, xxi, 4, 5, 14, 17, 42,
   50–51, 58, 126
Bowling, Roger, 45
Bradley, Jerry, 117–18, 122–25
Bradley, Owen and Harold, 59
"Branded Man," 49
Brandt, Paul, 36
Bransounds, xxiii
Broadcast Music Incorporated (BMI),
   xix, 11, 31, 71, 73, 79
Brooks, Garth, xx, 4–5, 12, 44, 50, 51,
   58, 75–76, 99, 129, 134
Brooks & Dunn, 51, 119
Brown, Ruth, 59
Brown, Sawyer, 50, 56, 108–9
Brown, T. Graham, 50
Browne, Jackson, xxi
Bruce, Ed, 41
Bryant, Boudleaux and Felice, 70
"Burned Like a Rocket," 61
"Burning Bridges," 106
Burr, Gary, 27, 28
Butler, Larry, 41–42, 44–45
"By the Time I Get to Phoenix," 50

Campbell, Glen, 50, 61
Capitol Records, xx, xxii, xxiii, 4–5, 14,
   42, 47, 48–58, 82, 126
Capitol-EMI, 50
Career Records, xxi, xxiii
Cargill, Henson, 60
Carlisle, Bill, 86
Carnes, Kim, 41
Carpenter, Mary Chapin, 37
Carter, Carlene, xxii
Carter, Deanna, 2, 51
Carter Family, 116
Cash, Johnny, 41, 88, 93, 123
cassettes, 97
"Cathy's Clown," 16, 117
"Cattle Call," 130

CBS Records, 91
CDs, 97
Chamberlain, Carson, 97
"Chantilly Lace," 87
Charles, Ray, 59–61
Chesney, Kenny, 133
"Chug-a-Lug," 87
Clark, Terri, 92, 93, 98
Clement, Jack "Cowboy," 74–75
Cline, Patsy, 128
Clovers, 59
CMI (Copyright Management, Inc.),
   71
"Coat of Many Colors, A," 130
Cochran, Anita, xxi, 25
Colter, Jessi, 118
Columbia Records, xxii, xxiii, 27, 92
"Come Early Morning," 75
Common Thread: The Songs of the Eagles,
   xxii
Confederate Railroad, xxi, 61–62
Conley, Earl Thomas, 118
Conrad, David, 91
"Could I Have This Dance," 17
"Country Sweetheart," 112
"Coward of the Country," 41
"Cowboy Man," 108
Cowboys, 86
Cramer, Floyd, 117
Curb, Mike, 55–57, 103–14; Congrega-
   tion, 106
Curb Records, xxiii, 3, 27, 56, 103–14
Cyrus, Billy Ray, 89, 92, 98, 133

"Daddy Never Was the Cadillac
   Kind," 62
Daily, Harold "Pappy," 87
"Dance, The": record, 50; video, 5
"Dang Me," 87
Daniels, Charlie, 5
Darrel, Johnny, 41
Davis, Linda, 8, 11
Davis, Paul, 57
Davis, Skeeter, 117
"Daytime Friends," 41
Dead Reckoning Records, xxiii
Decca Records, xxii, xxiii, 27, 43–44, 92

About the Author

Jennifer Ember Pierce grew up in southern Texas. In 1975, she graduated magna cum laude from Texas A&I University, majoring in political science and history. She entered graduate school at the University of Texas, majoring in criminal justice and administration. In 1988, she moved to Nashville.

Pierce has had her songs recorded by Johnny Cash with Hank Williams Jr., Janie Frickie, the Wood Brothers, and others. She has cowritten with several notable writers, including Garth Brooks.

Pierce is a writer and publisher member of the American Society of Composers, Authors and Publishers (ASCAP), a sterling member of the Country Music Association (CMA), a professional member of the Academy of Country Music (ACM), and a voting member of the National Academy of Recording Arts and Sciences (NARAS). She is also a member of Kappa Delta Pi, a national academic honor society, and Phi Theta Kappa, a national academic honor fraternity. She is the recipient of two Texas Music Appreciation Awards and is in *Who's Who in Entertainment 1992–93*. She has authored two books: *Breakin' Into Nashville: How to Write and Sell Country Music* (Madison Books, 1998) and *Playin' Around: The Lives and Careers of Famous Session Musicians* (Scarecrow Press, 1998).

Ashlw